The Turn Around

My Road of Repentance and Complete Surrender

21-DAY DEVOTIONAL

TAWANDA VAUGHN

THE TURNAROUND

The Turn Around
My Road of Repentance and Complete Surrender
21-DAY DEVOTIONAL

Copyright © 2023 Tawanda Vaughn

All rights reserved. No part of this book may be used or reproduced, stored in a retrieval system or transmitted in any way by any means, electronic, mechanical, photocopy, recording or otherwise without the prior permission of the author.

Scripture quotations, unless otherwise indicated, are taken from the Holy Bible, King James Version.

Cover: Enger Lanier Taylor – In Due Season Publishing ®

Interior Designer:
Enger Lanier Taylor – In Due Season Publishing ®

Published By: In Due Season Publishing ®
www.indueseasonpublishing.com
indueseasonpublishing@gmail.com

ISBN- 978-1-970057-17-1
      1-970057-17-3

THE TURNAROUND

TABLE OF CONTENTS

Day 1	Today, I Surrender Impatience	8
Day 2	Today, I Surrender to the Process of Surrender	13
Day 3	Today, I Surrender Money	16
Day 4	Today, I Surrender the Religious Misconceptions	20
Day 5	Today, I Surrender "My" Understanding	24
Day 6	Today, I Surrender My Story	27
Day 7	Today, I Surrender People	30
Day 8	Today, I Surrender Delayed Obedience	33
Day 9	Today, I Surrender The Spirit of Rejection	37
Day 10	Today, I Surrender Little White Lies	43
Day 11	Today, I Surrender Guilt	48
Day 12	Today, I Surrender How I See Myself	52
Day 13	Today, I Surrender Being "In" Love With Giving	56
Day 14	Today, I Surrender Fear	59
Day 15	Today, I Surrender Unforgiveness and the Residue	64
Day 16	Today, I Surrender The Way I Love	68
Day 17	Today, I Surrender The Hard Place	72
Day 18	Today, I Surrender Worrying	76
Day 19	Today, I Surrender to Letting God be God - Part 1	80
Day 20	Today, I Surrender to Letting God be God – Part 2	84
Day 21	Today, I Surrender Being Right	87

THE TURNAROUND

ACKNOWLEDGEMENTS

There were so many people who were instrumental, along the way, in getting this book out of me and into the world. Had I not believed GOD that I even had it in me, I wouldn't have ever started, let alone completed it. So I acknowledge that all glory and honor goes to Him because had I not ultimately believed HIM, it wouldn't have mattered what anyone else said.
THIS is Prophecy FULFILLED!!! Thank you Jesus!

But let patience do it's complete work, so that you may be mature and complete, lacking nothing.
James 1:4 KJV

Day 1

Today, I Surrender Impatience

"…Take This Cup From Me."

Luke 22:42

Some of you probably read this verse and completely judged Jesus. You probably asked yourself, how is He the Messiah and God's son struggling like that? Is this not the same one the Bible says He "volunteered" to come down to earth and complete the task staring Him in the face? Some of us don't even realize that Jesus wasn't, isn't, and will never be the only one to pose this question to God. We all have uttered this statement to Him as well, whether you know it or not, and if you haven't yet, keep living. Here's a perfect and personal example. One day, For *Self-Care Saturday* in my online Worship Class, we were challenged by our instructor to "pause" from something that day and to comment on what that something was. My response was, I'll be pausing from negative thoughts from the enemy. She challenged me to study Isaiah 50. In God's own ironic but not so ironic way, He used a verse in that chapter to show me something about myself that was completely different from what we were being challenged to do. In Isaiah 50:5, Isaiah is explaining his steadfast faith in his adversities, but here's where it gets good; in chapter 50:6, He says, "I offered my back to those who struck Me, and my cheeks to those who ripped my beard out of my face. Yet I didn't hide my face from those who humiliated and spit on me." Instantly I became emotional as the Holy Spirit reminded me how Jesus offered himself to physical and emotional torment and abuse. Though He struggled tremendously when the time came, He didn't turn away from His assignment.

Then I was reminded of Jesus's words in Luke 22:42, "Father, if you are willing, take this cup of suffering from me." God paused me right there and told me that is what I've repeatedly asked of Him when I've asked to be taken out of my previous season. Ironically not so ironic, right? Can you imagine my surprise? I'd gone to one passage of the Word to help me fight the enemy's attack on my thoughts, and God used that same Word to show me myself! When we're in something for so long, a season, circumstance, or situation, we tend to grow "weary," and I was very much in that position and state of mind. Proverbs 13:12 says, "Hope deferred makes the heart grow sick," which means discouraged or deep disrepair. Something you've been hoping and waiting for over an extended period can make your heart literally sick. But be not dismayed; God knows how far we can be stretched even and especially more than we do. He's not punishing you in this process; He's training and preparing you for a greater work, and for you to fight against this processing will only make you struggle more. How? The very "hope" that you are waiting to be fulfilled can make you feel like you're in a hostage situation simply because of your desire to get out of it too quickly. You will stay stuck and sick if God can't process you for the future assignment, mission, and calling. He will not place you in the "wilderness" without first preparing you to be able to fight and even kill the "wild" when they try to attack, and they will. Just ask David in 1 Sam 17:34-36. He explained to Saul what qualified him to fight and beat Goliath, the Philistine that was wreaking havoc and fear in the Israelite territory. He said to Saul that God had already prepared him for this fight. While he was tending his father's sheep, a lion and a bear would come and take a lamb from the flock. He went after them, and when they revolted against him, he struck and killed them and rescued the sheep out of their mouths.

Had he fought against God, teaching him to fight bigger and stronger enemies than him, he would've never been prepared to fight the "uncircumcised Philistine" and his army, who were referred to as giants! So my question to you is, do you really understand what you're asking when you ask God to take you out of trying storms and seasons? I broke into tears, and from a repentant heart, I asked him to reveal to me what would happen if He honored my request and removed me from it prematurely. Are you willing to ask God to reveal that to you? Can you handle looking at yourself in the light of God's truth (John 3:21)? I asked God to show me how much oil (wisdom and revelation from the Holy Spirit) I would waste or not receive because I aborted my assignment (Isa. 61:1)? How much wisdom will I lack by the end of this (Prov. 2:6, 3:13-18)? Whose lives will be affected because I didn't finish getting all I needed to help them (Isa. 40:31)? How much weight of Glory will I forfeit (2 Cor. 4:17)? Who will die if I don't finish this race (Acts 20:24)?

Are you able to handle knowing the truth of how your life and the lives of others who depend on you will look if you give up now? Do we really understand what you ask of God when you ask to be prematurely taken out of "suffering"? There are some lessons, pain, sufferings, tests, and storms that we can not go without experiencing if we want to be "Christlike"! Rom. 8:17 says, "And since we are his children, we are his heirs. In fact, together with Christ, we are heirs of God's glory. But if we are to share in His glory, we must also share in his suffering." So instead of complaining, we should take God at His Word that He will work everything out for our good (Rom. 8:28) and thus always cause us to triumph (2 Cor. 2:14). We have to stop rushing the process and start asking God for patience to endure (James 1:4, Ecc. 9:11), strength to go on (2 Cor. 12:9), and love that covers a multitude of sin and heartaches along the way (1 Pet. 4:8). I had to repent, and so should you! Well, that's my personal story/testimony; now, let's talk about yours.

A few years ago, the instructor of the Foundation Class at my church, Rev. Valerie Walker, said something so profound as she usually did. She said, "We give satan 20, 30, 40, and for some, 50 years of our lives, then we get saved and can't wait on God 24 hours!" Can you imagine the looks on our faces when she said that? All of us were guilty! How can we be so patient with the things of this world (sin) and then turn around and be so utterly impatient with God? His son suffered for us! Do you really think that God would make it easy for you? If you can't survive the pit, you won't be able to maintain being in the palace! Just ask Joseph in Gen. 37. God loves us so much that while we were yet sinners, he sent his only son to earth to suffer, become a curse, swap his righteousness for our filthiness and die for us. (Rom. 5:8) Let that sink in for a minute. What area(s) in your life do you struggle with being patient? List below the things that you are impatient with. For example, it can be children, husband/wife, job, living conditions, spiritual setbacks, etc.

_____
_____

Repeat after me...

God, I surrender my impatience of (repeat out loud all the things you wrote) to you today. I repent for being more patient with the things of the world than I am with you and the things of the Kingdom of Heaven. I surrender these things and ask that you burn them away by Holy Ghost fire until they are no more. Help me to let patience have its perfect work in me. Please help me to see the big picture. Help my desire to line up with the things that you desire. Help me to hate the things you hate and love the things you love. Even and especially, help me to remain diligent in this place of waiting for as long as it takes because your timing is perfect and best. In Jesus' mighty name. Amen.

"Father, if you are willing, please take this cup of suffering away from me. Yet I want your will to be done, not mine."
Luke 22: 42 NLT

Day 2

Today, I Surrender to The Process of Surrender

Surrender (Wikipedia) - willful acceptance and yielding to a dominating force and their will.

Surrender (Biblical) - "Dying to self," or the "emptying of self" to allow Christ to live through the believer.

     For some people, the word surrender is taboo, and no one wants to deal with it. They attach the same stigma to it as they do the words "obey" and "submit." But do you know that Jesus Himself also had to surrender? He surrendered to being beaten, physically and emotionally abused, talked about, spit on, lied on, and mistreated. He was stripped of his dignity, mocked, nailed to a cross, and left for dead! He subjected Himself to all of that for you and me! It is hard to believe; nevertheless, it's very true. Many believe in Jesus being the Son of Man but can't grasp the truth that He was fully God and fully human all at the same time! Because of the miracles, signs, and wonders He performed, they could see how He could be "A" God or some form of an entity with a great force behind Him. They could also believe in him being human because they could see him, talk to him, and touch Him, but believing He was 100% human while also being 100% God was inconceivable.

If you ever wondered why Jesus had to be fully like us, Heb. 2:17 NLT says, "Therefore, it was necessary for him to be made in every respect like us, his brothers and sisters, so that he could be our merciful and faithful High Priest before God. Then He could offer a sacrifice that would take away the sins of the people." Jesus's complete humanity was revealed in Luke 22:42. He was "now" burdened with the "process" of surrendering to the task that He had before Him so much that the Bible says He was "sorrowful unto death" and that His sweat was as "drops of blood" as He cried out, "Father, if you are willing, take this cup of suffering from me." If Jesus were fully God only, this part of scripture wouldn't have been necessary. After all, there wouldn't have been a struggle because nothing can ever make God struggle. He showed his full humanity in this moment, even though He knew what He had "voluntarily" come down to earth for. Oh, but when it got close to that time, He asked God to release Him of the task at hand. Knowing what He had to do, only a human would risk being bold enough to ask God to give them a "pass" on a hard assignment. Sounds familiar? But also in that moment, with the "help" of an angel from heaven who came and gave Him the strength He needed (Luke 22:43) to stay the course coupled with His obedience, He finished the assignment and the rest of that verse by saying, "Yet not as I will, but thine will be done." So if Jesus surrendered even while struggling with His father's predestined plan, we can't think it will be easy for us because anything you want to do to grow in your relationship with God starting with being obedient, the enemy will come for you and come hard. I can't tell you that it will be easy if you don't fight the process, but it'll be easier than you ever thought or imagined and worth it!

Repeat after me…

Father, I surrender _____ to you today. Help me to not make it harder on myself by fighting the process. You are the God of all flesh, you hold the King's heart in your hands. I give you permission to control this area(s) of my life and anything and anyone attached to it. I surrender my life to you to add, subtract, multiply, divide and change as you see fit. Have your way in me oh God. In Jesus' name, Amen.

"For you know the grace of our Lord Jesus Christ, that though he was rich, yet for your sake he became poor, so that you through his poverty might become rich."
2 Corinthians 8:9 NIV

Day 3

Today, I Surrender Money

"You doubt me when it comes to money." That's what the Holy Spirit said to me a few years ago. Over 10 plus years ago, I was going through so much financial turmoil. Our building was threatening foreclosure, and this was around the time when Obama had just created the program for home and property owners, just to give you a better timeline. I had "faith" that God would create a space for me to be one of the recipients of this program to lower my mortgage payments, but this is where we mess up. I prayed, and I "took Him at His Word." Did you catch that? He didn't send anyone to prophesy that this was for me. He didn't give me a confirmation on it, not even a sign. I just took Him at what was "written." The Word says, "God will supply all your need according to His riches in glory by Christ Jesus" (Phil. 4:19). I believed when His Word said, "Your Father knows exactly what you need even before you ask him" (Matt. 6:8). I also stood strong on Matt. 6:26 that says, "Look at the birds of the air, they don't sow, reap or store in barns, and yet your heavenly Father takes care of them. Are you not worth much more than they?" I stood on his Word and believed despite what others said, and guess what? It didn't happen! I was completely shocked that God didn't come through for me. How could this be? He's not short of his Word right? His promises are yes and amen, right? I cried out to God; WHAT HAPPENED? Why didn't this happen? You said ALL things are possible for those that "believe," so why didn't this work out for me? I was devastated. That was when I started doubting Him, and I didn't even know it. I asked, prayed, and believed what was written, but… Did I ever get an answer from God? Now, back to the moment, the Holy Spirit spoke to me. As I pondered further, I realized that God didn't lie to me. He simply just never responded. I realized in that moment that I just wanted what I wanted so bad that I leaned on the Word but didn't wait to get a "confirmed word." God speaks, reveals, confirms, and answers in many different ways, but are we really watching and listening, or do we really even care what He wants for/from us as long as He gives us what we want? Sometimes we ask God for things and never consider if it's what He wants for us, or if it's in His perfect will for our lives. Now here it is many years later, and He reveals to me that I doubt Him when it comes to money.

God didn't answer me because He knew I would have been out of his will if He had done what I wanted him to do. How? Because the future assignment He had for me required me to be in another place, that assignment has been fulfilled. So you see, not only did He reveal to me that I doubted him, but He also took me back to the exact place and day it started! Out of all the emotions I felt on that day, the feeling that trumped them all was love. I know, strange right? But honestly, the only thing I cried out of a repentant heart in that moment was, Father, thank you for loving me enough to tell me the truth about me!

Some of us can't handle hearing the truth, especially not about ourselves. But my prayer has always been, Father, show me myself the way you see me. Not the way my family, friends, my enemies, and even what I perceived about myself. I desire to see and know myself through the eyes of my Father and Creator. He risked it all to show us the truth because He loves us too much to leave us in bondage to anyone or anything! Not only does the truth set you free (John 8:32), it creates a path for obedience. Every moment since then, when it comes to money, I am intentional about making sure I don't move until He says.

There are times in our lives that God will put us in a position to remember not necessarily who He is, but who He's always been! So, in that moment, from the depth of a hard place, I had to remember and declare that God is still better than good to me, even when what I prayed for doesn't come to pass. Why? Because just like the three Hebrew boys in Daniel 3, my God will deliver me out of this, but even if He doesn't, he is able, and I'll never bow down to the enemy again. So, as you read, one of my enemies was lack. What is one of your enemies? Is it also lack? Is it doubt, trust issues, low esteem, self-hatred, etc.? Take a moment to think about it.

What is your "this" that you are waiting for God to make happen for you? Make sure you don't just take Him at what is written in His Word, but more importantly, actively and intentionally wait on an answer. Ask Him to reveal to you the areas in your life where you doubt Him? It could be the very area that is blocking what you are waiting on from coming to pass. You will be amazed to find out that, sometimes, where you think you have no doubt is the area that doubt has made it's home in your life. Now, let's do some work.

Spend ten minutes, after you ask Him, in complete silence. Just be still and say, "Speak Lord, your servant is listening (1 Sam. 3:7-11). Do this three times a day for a week. I know most of you don't have that kind of time, I understand. But at least make some time for God, and if you can't, then there lies the problem. So for those that can do the three times a day for seven days, do it, and for those that can't, then do one time a day for ten days. Furthermore, "me time" is crucially and equally as important as your personal and intimate time with just you and God. We do so much for others and neglect ourselves and especially God every time. Well, no more! The time to be restored is now, and that can only happen by intentionally making time for the Master.

14 "And this is the confidence that we have in him, that, if we ask anything according to his will, he hears us: 15 And if we know that He hears us in whatever we ask, we know that we have the requests which we have asked of Him."
1 John 5:14-15

Day 4

Today, I Surrender The Religious Misconceptions

I want to ask why, but you're not supposed to "question" God. Sound familiar? This is one of the biggest misconceptions ever told. Not only is it not the truth, but it is extremely dangerous to our process of getting to know our Father in heaven. One day I was conversing with a friend, and we were sharing our frustrations from our current season. She shared a conversation that she recently had with God about all the things she was experiencing that were contradictory to His Word and to her being His daughter. She said, "God, I tithe, I sow, I give, I help...Where is my portion?" She didn't know that we voiced the same exact questions and concerns to God.

I honestly believe that the line between asking questions that cry out for wisdom and a deeper understanding of who God is and His ways verses questions that are asked only to avoid or delay our obedience, asked from a prideful heart, and asked for the sole purpose of seeking validation from man (people), is simply a matter of motive and the posture of our hearts (1 Sam. 16:7). His Word says, "Let God be true and every man a liar." There are very specific promises God is waiting to fulfill in the lives of those who ask. Matthew 7:7 says, "ask, and it shall be given." Mark 11:24 says, "Whatever you ask for in prayer, believe that you have already received it, and it will be yours." James 1:5 says, "If any of you lacks wisdom, let him ask of God, who gives generously to all without finding fault, and it will be given to you." and the simplest put yet most profound is in James 4:2, "…You have not because you ask not." These are just scratching the surface of God's many scriptures specifically giving us permission to ask.

In the reverse, if you are asking questions that go against His will and his already ordered steps for your life, you probably shouldn't look for your request to be granted. Why? Because He cannot go against His own will and Word. BUT…Sometimes, God will give you what you're asking for to show you just how bad it is for you and to refocus you. Now, this is not the norm, but it has happened. God is a staunch protector of His Word and His people, so if you have already asked and received an answer and continue asking because it wasn't what you wanted to hear, you will cause self-inflicted suffering. Just ask the Israelites in 1 Sam. 12:19. They begged God for a King, and God told them that they didn't need one. Why? Because He was their King. But they wanted a King simply because their enemies had one. They felt they would be more intimidating if they had a physical King in the natural that their enemies could see, forgetting all the power God had already displayed from the spirit realm. So God eventually gave them what they asked for, which was a major fail! This is a classic case of when competition goes horribly wrong. Let's do one more for good measure. It's one of my own personal stories that I think will help drive things home for you. Have you ever heard anyone pray, "Thank you for protecting me from dangers seen and unseen?" I've prayed that quite a few times, but I went beyond thanking Him for it on this particular day and asked Him to reveal the unseen things to me. Within two weeks after praying that, I had four dreams, and all of them had two common occurrences; loved ones or myself being victims and potential victims of sexual assault and the other was me physically fighting. None of them left me with reason for concern after I woke up except the last one, and I couldn't shake it. I wasn't necessarily fearful, but I wanted to know if I needed to be on alert. So, I asked God what was the meaning of them all, especially the last one.

A few minutes later, the Holy Spirit reminded me of my prayer about revealing to me the unseen things. He told me that fighting in the dreams wasn't me. It was Him fighting off and blocking the impending danger that the enemy was trying to send to my family and me. He was protecting us in the spirit realm before it had a chance to reach us in the natural! ISN'T THAT GOOD? If I were still operating out of religion and not a relationship (there's a difference), I wouldn't have asked God to show me because I wouldn't have known or even believed that I could! Now, if that isn't enough to make you ask God to deliver you from that religious mindset that is holding you in bondage, I don't know what else will work. So now that I've given you a better understanding of what questioning or asking God for something really entails let's do some work.

What are some things that you have wanted to ask God but were afraid to because you thought you couldn't? It doesn't have to all be recent; it can also be something from years past. It doesn't matter how big or small. Get a pen and a piece of paper, you can even use your notepad on your phone. Think of three things you always wanted to ask, take a deep breath, ask Him, sit there in silence for twenty-one minutes and write down what He says. You can ask all at once or one at a time. Be warned; the enemy doesn't want you to get an answer because an answer from God is your weapon against Him! So, He will use anything and anyone to be a distraction.

Say this prayer out loud; Father, as I submit myself to you and resist the devil, your Word says he has to flee. Remove all distractions, tricks, and tools of the enemy right now, and thank you for covering me as I seek you. In Jesus' name, I pray, Amen.

You may get an answer right away or receive it later, but at least you would have broken the spirit of fear and religion that says you can't question God. Remember, He isn't like us. He speaks in many different ways. So even if you don't get an answer when and where you asked, don't count Him out or doubt what you've read today. Your answer may come while you're in your house, driving in your car, taking a stroll, or even during a business meeting. Ask God not to let you miss the signs. Watch and listen.

5 Trust in the LORD with all your heart, and do not lean on your own understanding. 6 In all your ways acknowledge him, and he will make straight your path. Proverbs 3:5-6 ESV

Day 5

Today, I Surrender "My" Understanding

"Don't trade in what you know about God for what you don't understand." Lasandra Hutchinson

What does it mean "don't lean on your own understanding"? To get an understanding means the ability to comprehend from a different perspective or to be sympathetically aware, tolerant, and forgiving of other people. So, to not lean on your own understanding is basically to not criticize or judge a person or situation based on what you perceive, assume, or heard, but based on the "truth." There were so many things that happened in my life that I didn't and still don't understand. One situation rocked me to my core and left me heartbroken, confused, and manifested thoughts of whether God even loved me. Almost 20 years ago, I experienced heartache and extreme betrayal, and I was emotionally wounded so profoundly that it emerged into physical pain in my body. I can honestly say that I'm completely healed from everything I endured at that time. Still, I've just recently learned that in some situations, what we believe we have forgiven and healed past, we either have some residue left of it or it isn't healed or forgiven at all. It's just "asleep" deep inside us. Unlike the story of Sleeping Beauty, where the beautiful young Princess falls into a deep sleep, and the only way to wake her is a kiss from her true love. Well, for me, I don't won't it to wake up! I want that mess to stay asleep! I mean dead and never to be resurrected, but that's not the way God works. He's raising up whole, healed, delivered, anointed, and authority-carrying overcomers who won't bleed all over the captives they're sent to help set free (Luke 4:18)!

Now back to this "dead" situation. I was confused and traumatized. Surely God knew how this person was going to treat me. I was angry and felt like God couldn't love me because if he did, he wouldn't have placed this person in my life to hurt me so deeply. I asked God, how can you love them more than you love me? That had to be what it was, right? I tried with everything in me to understand what good God was going to bring out of so much pain, but, to no avail, I came up with nothing. It became harder and harder to pray, and when I did, I was a bitter, broken mess. We had been so close before then, so why would God jeopardize us? I just had no understanding. All I knew was that I was hurting, and as far as I was concerned, it was God's fault! Surely, He didn't love me.

Well, I came to realize that was the furthest thing from the truth! He did in fact, love me beyond my finite and limited human mind, and heart could ever comprehend, and guess what? He also loved the person that hurt me as well. Yes! God loves the people that hurt us too. I know. It's a hard pill to swallow, but it's the truth anyhow. He doesn't show favoritism (Acts 10:34). He causes His sun to rise on the evil as well as the good (Matt. 5:45). He doesn't just show grace and mercy to you. He offers it to everyone! It really is good news, as hard as that may be to hear. Also, believe it or not, that person is now one of my closest friends and has been for years. Needless to say, God checked me about how I felt, in love, of course, and I gave Him a very teary-eyed repentance. I had to repent. He told me that my own disobedience led to my pain but that the pain was purposed! Imagine that. God used what the enemy meant for evil and turned it for my good (Gen. 50:20). How, you may ask?

A little over a year later, someone came into my life going through the same circumstances I had just gotten out of, and God used me to help them. You may not understand why God allows certain things to happen, but I'm a living witness that He doesn't do or permit anything to happen without a purpose. He's a strategic, intentional God who loves us so much. Nothing you can ever do will or can change that (Rom. 8:35-39). So now, let's do a self-check.

Are you in this situation now, or have you found yourself in it before? You had no understanding of what or why something happened to you or a loved one, and you accused God of being unjust! Were you ever honest with God about how you felt, and if you were, were you bitter and angry like I was? I want you to stop what you're doing right now and tell God you're sorry for how you mishandled him in your lack of understanding. Ask Him to help you to trust Him from here on out no matter what happens. Ask Him to give you understanding of that situation again and if you've never asked before, take a deep breath. Come on, breathe! Then ask Him to reveal the things that are asleep inside you that you thought you were healed from. Please, do not approach God as if He is the enemy. Instead, go to Him as His humble child seeking comfort, understanding, and wisdom. You may or may not get a response right then. Still, I promise that the peace that will flood you just from being able to ask without hindrance from anger and judgment is unbelievably liberating. You won't regret it even if you don't get an immediate response.

And they overcame him by the blood of the Lamb, and by the word of their testimony.
Rev. 12:11a

Day 6

Today, I Surrender My Story

February 13th, 1993 was the day I made one of the biggest mistakes of my life. I was 19 years old and I had an abortion. This decision led me on a downward spiral of guilt and shame. Forget talking to anyone about the emotional torment I was going through. I didn't want to be condemned anymore than I was already doing to myself. The father of the child didn't want me to do it so his pain led him to lash out at me. I was called a "baby killer", "child murderer", and other hurtful names. I didn't fight with him because that is how I felt about myself! Don't get me wrong; he had every right to be hurt and even angry. He begged me not to do it. Sometimes we only think about how the woman feels in this situation, and we completely ignore the man's pain. Just because they don't show or voice it doesn't mean they weren't affected. Sure, he could've found a better way to express his pain, but how many of you know how to react properly to something so emotionally damaging?

Unfortunately, his pain created an atmosphere for him to attack me routinely, using that as ammunition, and I was so guilt-ridden that I allowed myself to be shut down every time. My shame led me to pray daily for forgiveness from God and my child, starting with the very moment I woke up on the operating table. But how could God forgive such a thing? How could He love me after killing the gift He had placed inside me? I couldn't conceive it. One morning, years later, I woke up with it heavy on my heart which usually didn't happen because I always prayed before I went to bed, but this day was different. The atmosphere in my room was different. I can't explain it other than to say there was a sense of calm, peace, and stillness that I had never experienced before, and my room was filled with a thinned-out cloudiness. So, I started that morning as I did nightly, praying and asking for forgiveness, and out of nowhere, I heard, "I forgave you the very first time you said I'm sorry." At that very moment, my entire being exhaled. God healed and delivered me from guilt, shame, and condemnation. It was like my heart had taken a deep sigh of relief. The burden had been lifted, and I felt it leave! I broke down in tears and began to thank God for his undeserved forgiveness and mercy. In that moment, He freed me from what led me to torture myself and be tortured for years. He had forgiven me the very first time I said I was sorry. Can you imagine how much grief I could've saved myself? Of course, a few days after that the enemy tried to lure me back into condemnation but with my new found freedom, however, this time it went a little bit differently. A conversation with the father started off normal and ended up in an argument out of nowhere as it often did, and of course, the hurtful names ensued. Quite to his surprise, my response was alarming to him. I literally laughed out loud. He was so taken back that he paused and then asked, "What's so funny? You're proud to be a baby killer? It's funny to be a child murderer?" Completely unbothered, I told him, "You can't hurt me with that anymore. God has forgiven me, and as long as He has forgiven me, that's all that matters!" I had shut him down, for the first time since I had the abortion. It was FINALLY over! He could no longer silence me, and he never brought it up again after that day. I have often prayed that he receives the same healing and deliverance that I did. I wasn't the broken woman that I was all those other times. I had finally stood up for myself and took back my power, and so can you!

One of the ways God uses us is through our most painful circumstances. Those hidden secret events that we feel too ashamed to share. God uses our stories to help others be set free, and that's exactly what He did with mine. Our story is the testimony that Rev. 12:11 is talking about that helps us overcome the enemy. So don't withhold what God wants to use. You never know whose life you will impact. Someone is waiting to hear your testimony, so tell it. Now let's do some work.

What story are you withholding out of fear, shame, and guilt that God can use? Are you willing to let God first heal your heart and then deliver you so that He can use your story to help set someone else free? Someone reading this right now has prayed for God to use them and in a major way. What if one of those significant ways He desires to use you is through what you're withholding, your story.

Repeat after me….

I _____, surrender the guilt, shame and pain of what I went through to God, who is the lover and healer of my soul. God I surrender my story of _____ to be used by you to help someone else. I ask that you prepare my mind and heart and remove fear so I can walk in obedience to your leadership. In Jesus' name. Amen

30 Love the Lord your God with all your heart and with all your soul and with all your mind and with all your strength.' 31 The second is this: 'Love your neighbor as yourself. There is no commandment greater than these."
Mark 12:30-31

Day 7

Today, I Surrender People

Do you know someone who lives much of their life caring about what other people say and think about them? I used to be that person. Yes, I used to be a "people pleaser." People pleasers are the nicest, most helpful people you may ever meet. They hardly ever say "no" to anyone about anything. In fact, they spend most of their time doing things for others more than themselves! Usually, the root of this "disease to please" is the spirit of rejection which leads to low self-esteem, insecurity, and the need to compare yourself to anyone you think is better or different than yourself. They usually deem themselves as less or least compared to most, and for some of you who are still in this struggle, here are some words of wisdom. Being a people pleaser is dangerous, self-destructive, and completely disrupts your relationship with God. How? Because until you make the decision to be submitted and committed to God first, you will always feel the need to please the people that you can see more than God who you can't see.

In Mark 12:30-31, when questioned by the Sadducees about which is the most important commandment, Jesus answered and said, "Love the Lord with all your heart, soul, mind and strength and love your neighbor as yourself." God is first not only because He is the creator of all things, including you and me, but also because in Him is where you discover who you are. In God lies your worth and your true identity. There was a time in my life when it literally hurt me to say no to people. It didn't matter what it was for. One day, a very good friend of mine shared a fascinating story of when she was a child attending Catholic school. The nun gave the class a nugget of wisdom that helped shift my life. Those words were, "the For You is understood." I took that little five-word statement and applied it to every area of my life. Allow me to explain; When someone asks you for something, it doesn't matter what it is; even if you have it, there's no further explanation needed after the word, no, because the "For you is understood." In other words, I have it, but I don't have it for you! As hard as it was for me to come out of that destructive mindset, I first learned how exhilarating saying no was when I gave my life back to God twenty-two years ago. I learned that saying yes to God was saying yes to myself, which left very little room for a yes for anyone else.

I also learned that "No" is an anointed word. It can sometimes carry the same weight as wisdom, discernment, and some of the other spiritual gifts. Ask Jesus in Matt. 4:1-11. He not only fought the devil with the Word of God, but He also fought him with a two-letter word, No.

So in closing, saying no at the "appropriate" times sets you free to love, give, live, have peace, be confident in, and reach for goals and dreams for yourself! Many won't understand when they start hearing no if they aren't accustomed to it coming from you, but that's ok; that's not your business! Be ready for people to change towards you. It literally frustrates people when they can't use and take advantage of you any longer. They will become mean, standoffish, and in some cases, disrespectful, but again that's not your business. Now let's do some work.

Start creating boundaries. The enemy hates when you protect your peace, personal/professional space, home, or anything else concerning you! The devil absolutely HATES when he can't wreak havoc in your life anymore. So, it literally stifles him, and he eventually moves on, but beware he's coming back, dressed up and presenting himself in a new and different way. Still, it's that same old "familiar" spirit. Why? Because he can't do anything new. He's an imitator, not a creator. Think about it; there's nothing for him to create; God has done it all (John 1:3)! So what are two things that you always say yes to when people ask for it? It doesn't matter who asks - husband, child, mother, father, friend, boss, sibling, etc. Whether it be time, energy, money, sex, advice, listening to pity party stories, giving them a ride, or doing anything they can do for themselves. Even the things they can't do on their own doesn't mean it has to be done by YOU!

Decide on two things and ask God to help you say no and watch him work (Luke 12:12, 21:15). If you can only decide on one right now, that's fine. There will be an overwhelming sense of guilt for some of you, which is normal. Anything you're not used to doing will feel uncomfortable; it's also a trick of the enemy to keep you stuck and bound. So fight through that. Ask God to remove that feeling and replace it with his peace and confidence (1 John 5:14, 2 Chron. 32:8). Once you get used to saying no, that uncomfortable, guilty feeling will start to dissipate, and you will wonder why it ever took you so long to do it. Also, ask God to give you balance with your new freedom because you don't want to start saying no to everything! Some things still need a yes. Ask God to reveal it to you if you're unsure which is which.

1:1 The LORD gave a word to Jonah son of Amittai...3a Instead, Jonah ran from the LORD....he bought his ticket, then got on the ship and sailed away to escape the Lord...17 The LORD sent a big fish to swallow Jonah, and Jonah was inside the fish for three days and three nights...2:1 From inside the fish Jonah prayed to the LORD his God. 10 And the LORD commanded the fish, and it vomited Jonah onto dry land. Jonah 1:1, 3, 17, 2:1,10

Day 8

Today, I Surrender Delayed Obedience

"Delayed obedience is disobedience!" Rick Warren

Have you ever heard that statement before? Well, I have, and the first time I did, it pricked me to my core, but nothing prepared me for the day that GOD said it to me. One day, a few years ago, I received a text from one of the ministers at my church. The text simply said, "God told me to tell you that He's waiting to gift you with a car, but He can't because you're not prepared." I hadn't been behind the wheel of a car in twenty plus years, and I was ok with that. When I did drive, I hated everything about it; the fear, stress, and having to be on constant alert. It was all too much for me. So, I stopped and never desired to do it again. Of course, I knew what the text meant because I had dream after dream of me driving, so I concluded that they were a setup for what was to come. But, fear and not wanting to do it led me to procrastinate, and conviction and a warning followed towards the end of that same year. I knew without a doubt that God was not playing with me. So after a few more months of procrastination, I took the written test on a whim, and I passed. A couple of weeks later, I got my permit, and it was time to find a driving school. I knew if I took the time to look for a driving school based on what "I could afford," I would never step out on faith and complete my assignment. So I said, "God, I'm going to type in the top five driving schools, and you direct me to the one you want me to go with."

Shortly after that, God told me that a young lady who I had been following on social media for over three years at that time was my mentor. I knew what position prolonged hesitation had put me in before, so I immediately emailed her and set up our first session. All of the extra responsibilities put me under a financial strain, and in my typical humanity, I blamed God. "God, you told me to get my license. I didn't want to drive. You told me that this person was my mentor. You knew what I was working with. I trusted that you would provide what I needed. I didn't ask for any of this!" I heard God clearly say, "No! It was your delayed obedience that put you in this financial strain." My knees buckled as He gave me visions and timelines of if I had just done what was told of me, when it was said, I would've completed the driving lessons long before He told me about my mentor, and the two extra financial responsibilities would've never collided with each other. This was all my fault, not God's! I did this to myself. I don't understand why we blame God every time something doesn't go as we thought it should, but I know that God is faithful even in our failure to move swiftly.

I learned a very valuable lesson from Jonah. You might say, well, the lesson you should've learned is not to delay your obedience to God, and that's true, but what I learned more than that is that every delayed obedience is not someone running from God. Sometimes it's fear, insecurities, having no confidence in your capabilities to do what was presented to you successfully, etc. Jonah ran from God because He wanted Nineveh to receive God's judgment. As far as he was concerned, they deserved it! But again, what I learned more than anything else about Jonah's story is that God knew that he would run away from his assignment, so God already had a plan in motion that would put Jonah right back in position to do the right thing, be obedient (Deut. 7:9). That's what He did for me as well. Sometimes, we must suffer some of the consequences of disobedience to avoid doing it again. I repented, and if you've ever been here, so should you! Now let's get to the root of this thing.

What are you delaying in your life? What keeps you from moving when you know you're supposed to and/or especially when you know it's God? Is it fear of failure, rejection from people, fear of not being qualified or worthy, or fear of success? Yes, you can have an equal and even surpassing fear of success as you do failure, but 2 Tim. 1:7 says, "For God has not given us a spirit of fear; but of power, of love, and of sound mind (self-control)." God knows that fear, if we allow it, will hold us in bondage for so long that the very thought of stepping outside of it and into "His" freedom will drive us right back into our holding cell, thus placing ourselves in what feels like an eternal state of stagnation. So today, declare and decree that fear will no longer stop you from becoming who you were predestined to be or stop you from doing what you're supposed to do RIGHT THEN!

Repeat after me...

God, I am yours! You created me for a purpose and greater works, unlike anything that my feeble, finite mind can fathom. I surrender my fears, doubts, worries, insecurities, and even my understanding and lack thereof to you. Mold and shape me into the fearless person that you created me to be. Help me to learn, apply and walk in the power, love, and self-control that your Word says you have given me. Lead me by your truth on the path of freedom that I have never experienced before, and help me stay focused on you and nothing else until I see the finish line. In Jesus' name, I pray. Amen

So God created mankind in his own image; in his own image God created them;
he created them male and female.
Gen. 1:27 ISV

Day 9

Today, I Surrender The Spirit of Rejection

There was a time in my life when all I liked about myself was my smile and my heart and nothing else. I was different in every way from my siblings and not just in looks but also in our ways, our thinking, how we dressed, what we liked, who we liked, and so on. I was just different. You don't know anything about genetics and bloodlines when you're a child. We didn't have the same father, and for a time, I was the only one that didn't. God sent my mom from Chicago to Florida to conceive me. It was all orchestrated by Him. When I was a month old, she returned to Chicago, and eventually got back with my oldest sister's father, and my little sister was born six years later. God knows what two DNA's He wants to put together to create His masterpiece, and nothing, not even distance, time or location will prevent His plan from coming to fruition.

THE TURNAROUND

YOU ARE NOT A MISTAKE! I felt like I needed to scream that to some of you to help it sink in because the enemy has lied to you just like he did me, and tricked you into believing this for so long that it will take some hard-core proof, in your mind, to change that. Well, the proof is in Jeremiah 1:5. Allow me to break it down in my own words; God said, "I knew you before I placed you in your mother's belly. Before you were born into this world and anyone had a chance to warp your thinking or your identity to try and make you fit in where they thought you should fit, I had already created you to be different." That is what I hear when I read that scripture. So the fact that God created you to be different, even from your own siblings and family members, should help you want to learn to love yourself for who you really are! I'm not talking about the misguided and twisted you that you were made to believe that you are; I'm talking about the you that God created you to be. The you that He created in His very own image according to Gen. 1:27. So the next time you start to doubt why you're here, remember that you are here because you were on God's heart, mind, and in His plan for a very special and specific purpose. God used the sin of my parents to get me here. Yes, even our sin is in His plan to get us born into the world in His proper, divine, and predestined time.

It's easy to see yourself in/with the proper perspective when you feel like you're equally loved within your home, but when favoritism is shown, it distorts your perception, opens doors to rejection, and the child starts to feel less than. It can also create low self esteem and an extreme feeling of low self worth. Favoritism creates mental and emotional damage and leads the child to feel the need to always try to be and do things "perfectly" to gain the affection, attention, and validation that's rightfully due them from birth! They then take all of that brokenness outside of the house and seek and search for anything and anyone that will give them what they're missing, and it's usually found in the most toxic people and the most physically damaging things. Love is an action word (1 John 3:18), but it's also learned. Most people can identify with Joseph and his personal story in Gen. 37, but I can identify more with his brothers. Joseph was loved, favored, and treated like the golden child. His brothers were disregarded, forgotten, and they only had the attention of each other. Sure their father took care of their basic needs, but the extra love, individual attention, validation, and confirmation that Joseph received, they didn't get. Rejection makes you think that someone is doing something to you and saying something about you that they're not saying or doing! It literally warps how you see and hear. I personally don't believe that Joseph was bragging to his brothers about his dreams. I believe that he was simply sharing them, maybe even trying to get their assistance in helping him figure out what the dreams meant. But because they were rejected, they took his sharing as bragging and him being arrogant when he really wasn't. Do I think he talked too much? YES! But that's what young people do. You have to remember that Joseph was much younger than his siblings, so he was doing what young, immature people do, not to mention he had no filter because he was allowed to "express himself" and his feelings in a way that I'm sure his brothers were not.

    Here's a very personal example. A friend of mine was so broken from rejection that it led her to take everything I said, including me expressing my feelings about anything, as me accusing and blaming her of something. One day I was having a moment. You know, it was just one of those days. I put up a post on Facebook that simply said, "I'm so glad that God counts tears as prayers." After reading that, she came to me and, in the most uncompassionate, most irritated voice and said, "What's wrong with you?" I was so taken back by her tone that I didn't even want to share, so I simply said, "Just not having a good day." Again in the same unconcerned, inconsiderate tone, she said, "Well, it happens," and basically, but not her exact words, she said that I should get over it. Now someone who loves and cares about how you feel would read something like that and want to comfort you, but she assumed that post was me accusing her of being the reason I felt how I felt.

Rejection distorts your hearing, thinking, reasoning, perception, and perspective about many things. Do people often tell you that you misunderstand what they say? Do you hear or read something that's not even being said? Is your point of view so warped that it makes you see something a different way than what's actually happening? Are you always on the defense? Do you always feel like everyone is attacking you or falsely accusing you of something? Then you are probably dealing with the spirit of rejection. There are mild to extreme cases of it. Mine was on the milder side, thank God, but I possessed a few of these traits. For those that know without a shadow of a doubt what spirit you have been operating out of, and yes, rejection is a spirit, let's do some work because until we deal with the issue, we can't overcome it! Even for those who just found out in reading this, this exercise is for you. Let's go!

God used my former spiritual mentor Markita D. Collins to go across the world to help set the captives free. In one of her events in L.A., she had us do this exercise, and I'm telling you, by doing this, rejection literally lost its grip on me from that day forward. But of course, like anything else, there was still a process of maintaining my deliverance that I had to go through. God led me to modify it, but it's the same concept.

Draw a door with your finger. It doesn't have to reach high or wide, just enough for you to fit through it. You don't have to open it because the door is already open if you're dealing with rejection or any other spirit. The drawing of the door is just what we're using as a symbol of the thing/place that we're walking out of that's been keeping you bound and keeping you from stepping into freedom on the other side. Now, the enemy will try and make you think that this little "fake act" that I'm about to tell you to do is nothing more than a useless motion, and he'll try to convince you that I'm the liar! How do I know this? Because he tried it with me as well.

Don't listen to anything that he says! Some of you may even struggle with knowing if it's the enemy's voice or God's. Let me say this if the voice is trying to keep you from walking through the door, it's the devil! On the other hand, if you feel a push, hear words of encouragement, or even feel the strength to walk through it, it's God! When you're ready, walk through that door. Did you do it? How do you feel? Some of you may feel a degree of anxiety and fear afterward; that's normal! Some of you may even feel like nothing happened, but it did, and that's normal as well.

You have now stepped into a place that you're unfamiliar with, and anything new can be scary and intimidating. Don't go back through the door! Instead, do what I did, turn around and motion with your arm to slam it shut and turn the imaginary lock so that it's never opened again! That means you have to do the work to keep the door shut. This is what we call a prophetic action. Because rejection is a spirit, you have to be freed from it in the spirit realm. So you've just prophetically acted out in the natural what you are closing the door on in the spirit. Some of you may have to slam the door several times, and when you get sick and tired of being sick and tired, take both your hands and imagine you have a hammer in one and nails in the other and swing! I mean, go around the entire door until you feel a release or until you get tired. Whichever comes first. Remember, It's God's responsibility to send the healing, but it's our responsibility to accept it, believe it, and maintain it. So again, how do you feel? Do you feel lighter, angry, free, or scared? It's ok. Sit down and give yourself time to process what just happened. The enemy will say, "So what now; you know nothing really happened, right?" Pay him no attention.

Repeat after me...

God, I just took one of the biggest steps of my life, to be free to do your will and allow you to have your way in me. I surrender the door that I just walked through to you and every step that I take in this new place moving forward. Lead me and guide me by your spirit so that I never go back and give me the wisdom to now deal with the process of walking in my healing and deliverance. In Jesus' name. Amen

16 There are six things that the Lord hates, seven that are an abomination to him: 17 haughty eyes, a lying tongue, and hands that shed innocent blood, 18 a heart that devises wicked plans, feet that make haste to run to evil, 19 a false witness who breathes out lies, and one who sows discord among brothers.
Proverbs 6:16-19 ESV

Day 10

Today, I Surrender Little White Lies

"YOU CAN'T HANDLE THE TRUTH!"

Most of you remember this famous line from the 1992 movie A Few Good Men. Nevertheless, it's one of the truest statements ever made. Why? Because for some, the truth hurts. It's not that they can't handle it in and of itself; what they can't handle is the pain that comes from knowing the truth! This is why some people would rather be lied to. Do you believe that? I know that's an "eye-opener" for some of you. It probably even made some of you uncomfortable, but it's true. Did you know that the truth is usually "hidden" in "plain sight?" This means it's not really hidden; you choose not to see it, acknowledge it, or you need a push in the right direction that leads you right to it.

Have you ever heard the quote, "If you go looking for something, you'll find it"? Well, it's true, and sometimes what we're looking for we really don't want to find. In fact, we're actually hoping and praying that we don't find what we already know is the truth. Why? Because knowing the truth brings pain. Sometimes, unimaginable. In reverse, sometimes the truth comes when you're not looking for it at all! It just shows up, knocks on your door, and bam! It's standing right there in your face, and either you're going to let it in, embrace it and strategize on what to do next, or you close the door, put the deadbolt on, and pretend it doesn't exist.

John 8:32 says, "Then you will know the truth, and the truth will set you free." Did you hear that? The truth sets you free. So the question is, do you want to be free? If you don't, ignore this entire story. If you do, strap on your seat belt and enjoy the rest of your ride to freedom. Can you believe some people think that just because they admit from the beginning that they lie makes it ok for them to continue doing it? So it's ok to be a professed liar but you make no effort to be a former and repentant one! In other words, as long as they're honest about it, they don't have to change, but you lying to them is never acceptable. Do you know that God hates lying? Notice I didn't say He hates liars. He hates the sin, not the person. Prov. 12:22a says, "Lying lips are an abomination to the LORD..." but most people think telling "small" lies is ok with God. I can assure you it's not! Small lies lead to medium size lies, and medium lies lead to big lies, all of which lead to the destruction of relationships and the reputations of those doing the lying and those being lied on. I've learned in my lifetime that a person who is habitual at wrongdoing towards others hates a taste of their own medicine.

For example, a liar hates to be lied to. A thief hates when someone steals from them. A deceiver hates to be deceived, and a snitch hates to be snitched on. However, I've also learned that there are many reasons why and how people become liars. Some people aren't really that way, nor do they want to continue being; they had to be for their own protection. Some people learned to be dishonest in order to survive! For some, they were going to be that way anyway because of a generational curse on their bloodline. They never had a chance. Yes, they can change it, but it's start was already predestined. Maybe these aren't good enough reasons for some, but sometimes we judge a person based on their current self and never take the time to know and understand their background story. Something happened to create that in them. Others are dishonest, and they're ok with it. They love the thrill of it, and they don't care who they hurt as long as the lie grants them the results they were seeking to gain. It's unfortunate but true.

    Honestly, I used to tell what I thought were harmless little white lies. I also told big ones as well. Have you ever noticed that the little ones made you feel worse than the big ones? The answer to that is simple. We think our reasons for the big ones are more acceptable than for the little ones, so it's easy to make an acceptable excuse for the big lies. That's why the little ones feel worse because there isn't a "good" reason for it. Some of us also think an exaggerated lie is better than an outright lie because it has some truth (Psalm 101:7 AMP). Let me assure you that none of it is acceptable, and it only leads to hurt, pain, and distrust of those closest to you. In life and death situations, telling the truth may do more harm than good, but those exceptions are not the norm! If you've found yourself in either category, little or big, then you need to do what I did and ask God to "Search me and know my heart: try me, and know my thoughts. Point out anything in me that offends you, and lead me along the path of everlasting life" (Psalm 139:23-24). I don't know about you, but I don't want anything I do or say to hinder me from "shining my light before people so that God gets the glory through my good works" (Matt. 5:14). I can gladly and honestly say that He heard my prayer and answered. He has nudged me when I'm about to say something untrue. When I've felt the urge to add some unnecessary stuff, He has stopped me in my tracks, and I'm grateful for that. I honestly don't know why I did it or where it came from, but I did what I needed to do to change it. All I can say is, thank

God for Jesus and for being an understanding and longsuffering(patient) God! Are you ready for him to change you? Well, let's do some work.

Are you a liar, or do you just tell little white ones? I know that question made some of you cringe, but this is the part where you get your help. One of the hardest things to do is to be honest with and about yourself! However, it's the only way to freedom. So this is not the time to be in denial or shrink back. You've come this far, so let's make it to the end together. I want you to think back to the very first time you lied. For some of you that may be too far to go back, ask God to reveal it to you and its circumstances. He knows you better than you know yourself. Now, what happened that made you feel like you had to lie? Were you scared, nervous, or in fear for your life? Were you trying to gain the attention/affection of someone? Were you trying to land a job or position or keep from getting a whipping from your parents? Did you do it because you just wanted to or because you felt like you "had" no other choice? Did you like the way it made you feel or the relief it gave you when you didn't get hurt or in trouble, blocking any guilt you may have felt? Lying is a stronghold and a spirit. It is a trick of the enemy to make you feel like the only way to receive what you want is by not telling the truth. So let's do this; the next time you feel the urge to lie, in your head, ask God to help you resist the urge and stop talking! This will be jarring to the person or people listening because you may be asked to explain the abrupt silence. Still, it is better to explain honestly, "I'm just making sure I got it right before I finish," than to continue with the lie and make things worse if you're found out. Do this every time; then, when you are by yourself, say,

Father, I ask you to continue to remove anything that's not like you that's in me! Burn it up by Holy Ghost fire. Help me stop doing the things that you hate, and help me do the things that are pleasing to you. Lord, I thank you for being an ever-present help in my times of trouble. Thank you for leading me into all truths by your Holy Spirit, so I can resist the father of lies and make him flee as I submit to you. It is so, and so it is. In Jesus' name Amen

There is therefore now no condemnation for those who are in Christ Jesus.
Romans 8:1 KJV

Day 11

Today, I Surrender Guilt

Have you or a loved one ever experienced something so horrific and blamed yourself for it? That was me. Let me start by saying that not knowing who you are, and your true identity in God will help create an atmosphere of guilt unlike anything you've ever imagined or experienced. Allow me to explain. Years ago, when I was in my mid to late 20s, my family experienced something that rocked us to our core, a close family member was being molested. Now here's where not knowing who you are comes in. God had been showing me for quite some time that this was happening, but I thought it was either the devil trying to entice me to revert back to worrying or it was me and my overly protective, worst-case scenario thinking. So every time I had a vision, I blew it off. Well, one day, I got a knock at my door, it was two of my family members standing there crying, and I asked what was wrong? What I heard next made my knees buckle. "So and so has been raping me." I had to catch myself and keep it together because I knew I had to be strong at that moment, but everything in me was screaming, NOOOOOOOO! I grabbed them, held on for dear life, and said that everything would be ok. It was then that I realized that all those visions were God revealing to me what was happening, and I had no idea.

I blamed myself for years. What if God was showing me what was about to happen, and had I known, I could've prevented it! I felt as if it was my fault that they had to suffer this horrific act. If I had known who I was and what was inside of me and more importantly, how God speaks to me, even if I couldn't have completely prevented it, I could've stopped it from going on for so long. These thoughts were unbearable. After that, I went into a dark place, deep within myself. The guilt had utterly consumed me. Why didn't I know that it was God revealing this to me? I stayed in that dark place for years until God led me into his perfect peace one day. I was having one of "those days." I got on my knees and cried out for Him to forgive me. What I heard and felt next will stay with me for the rest of my life. He told me, "There is nothing for me to forgive because you didn't do anything wrong. It wasn't your fault." Those words comforted me so much that I felt a release in my body. Through His loving words, he brought me peace as only He could, and I was free from guilt and condemnation from that day forward, every time the enemy tried to take me back to that dark place, I reminded him of God's words just like Jesus did in Luke 4:1-13. God's Word is our weapon! So let me ask, are you going through something you're blaming yourself for, are you ready to let it go? Are you prepared to be free? Have you ever experienced God's peace before? It's not to be confused with the world's peace. I'm talking about true peace that only comes from heaven (Phil. 4:7), and there is absolutely nothing that can compare to it. Are you ready to walk in His peace? Well, let's go.

What is it that you blame yourself for? Do you know that there's absolutely nothing we can say or do that God won't forgive? I know that's hard for some of you to hear, it was once hard for me as well, but I came to find out and believe that it's nothing short of the truth! There is absolutely nothing you can ever do that is beyond God's saving grace and the one and only thing that God's Word says is an unforgivable sin is found in Mark 3:28-29. Everything else is unconditionally forgivable. He showed us how much He loved us over 2,000 years ago when he sent His only begotten son to die for us while we were still sinners (Rom. 5:8). Do you believe it? Sometimes it's hard for us to believe that such a big God can be so loving, forgiving, compassionate, and merciful, but it's the truth. Are you tired of doing life YOUR way, and you're ready to let God have control from this day forward? 2 Peter 3:9 says, "The Lord isn't really being slow about his promise, as some people think. No, he is being patient for your sake. He does not want anyone to be destroyed but wants everyone to repent." He's waiting on you! That's how much He loves you. Are you ready to learn how to love Him back and receive the forgiveness his son died for you to have (Psalm 103:3)?

If you are ready for your life to change, you can do that right now, but only with and through Jesus. What you are about to read next is what is called a sinner's prayer. If you're not ready for this, then stop right now. But, if you are tired of doing life your way, you've tried everything and everyone and nothing has gotten better but worse. If you're sick and tired of being sick and tired and you're ready to give God a chance, then come on. Again, He's been waiting on you.

Repeat after me…

I _____ trade in my sins for God's forgiveness. I believe that He sent His son to die and be raised for ME and for no other reason than He loves me. I surrender myself and man's rejection of me and receive that God has already and has always accepted me. Today I accept Jesus as my Lord and Savior, and I permit Him to come into my heart and life to take full control. I ask that you help, lead, and guide me as I start my new journey in your will. If you have said this, you are now saved! YEP! It's that simple (Rom. 10:9-10). Now embrace your new life (2 Cor. 5:17), ask God to lead you to a church home, and ask Him to send people into your life that will help cultivate and bring out what's in you. I love you, and I'm so proud of you. Welcome to the family.

But if you look carefully into the perfect law that sets you free, and if you do what it says and don't forget what you heard, then God will bless you for doing it.
James 1:25 NLT

Day 12

Today, I Surrender How I See Myself

    I was having a conversation with a young lady one day who was struggling with how she looked because of the scars on her face. Now, she didn't have scars in a real sense; that's just what she called the blemishes she had as a result of a mild skin disorder. I remember her saying, "I wish I had your skin. I would love to look in the mirror every day! You have great skin." As I listened to her, I got quiet because I started feeling extremely emotional. I fought through my emotions enough to say to her, "If you think the only reason you're not pretty is because of your blemishes, then you don't want to hear my story or want my skin." She said, "Why not? Your skin is beautiful. You should never have a problem with looking in the mirror." Man, she was not ready for what I was about to say.

    I told her, "I've always had nice skin, this is true, but there was a period of time when I was your age and younger, I never looked in the mirror because I didn't like what I saw." She said, "But Why? Your skin is flawless!" No longer able to control my emotions, with cracking in my voice and a face full of tears, I said, "Because I didn't see my face, what I saw staring back at me was rejection, low self-esteem, unworthiness, etc. You see your blemishes. I saw the emotional wounds inside of me. I saw a person who felt unloved, undesirable, undeserving, and unworthy. So you see, even though I've never had blemishes or scars as you call them, what I saw were the inner scars and wounds that were on my heart! She was so outdone that all she could keep saying was, "Wooow." We never see ourselves the way others see us; never! They see strength and confidence. We see weakness and low self-worth.

    I hid my issues for years, or so, I thought. I know you see me on the back of this book all dolled up, looking like I've always had it all together, but I don't wear makeup at all in my everyday life, and I never have. I look a lot younger than my actual age, so I was used to getting prejudged because of that, and that played a significant part in me not liking how I looked. Crazy right? One day while at a monthly event I attended that was hosted by some extremely anointed and wisdom-filled friends who were able to see the real me. I'll never forget the woman of God said, "I know you don't like how you look, but you look different for a reason. God is preserving you for a special purpose, so stop comparing yourself to others." It was like someone turned on all the lights when she said that. I almost felt stupid for ever feeling that way, mainly because why would looking youthful ever be an issue? Actually, that is one of the other things I love about myself. But sometimes, I also felt like it was a curse because people treated me a certain way until I opened my mouth. Did you catch that? People will judge you and treat you a certain way because, to them, you "look" like you can be easily manipulated. That is until you open your mouth and wisdom comes spewing out. Then that's when they ask, "How old are you?" That's been the story of my life. Do you know that God will use you and the issues you have with yourself to reveal Himself to others?

A few years ago, one of my cousins had just bought a home and wanted everyone at her house for Thanksgiving. We didn't get together that often, but it was a good old time when we did. One of my favorite male cousins, who grew up as my little brother, was teasing me about how young I still looked, and the rest of the house jumped in as well. They were making their comments, joking and laughing, and a guy I had never seen before said, "We need to find out what you're doing to look that young at 45." My male cousin responded, "No! We need to get to know her God!" I remember thinking, "Flesh and blood did not reveal that to Him" (Matt. 16:17). Only God could take what I felt was sometimes a curse and use it to demonstrate to others that He is real! How did He do that, you ask? In that moment, my cousin knew that my preservation had nothing to do with me or anything I was doing! He saw the handiwork of God. It was supernatural! He revealed himself as a keeper and a preserver of those who wait on Him (Isa. 40:31)!

The majority of things we don't like about ourselves are the things that God highlights so that He can reveal Himself to others through us. He takes the good and what we consider bad and uses it to highlight Himself in us. God does that on purpose because He knows that "all sunshine and no rain creates a desert!" How will you ever know God as a heart fixer if your heart has never been broken? How would you ever know Him as Jehovah Jireh (God who provides) if you were never in need or had never experienced lack? How would you ever know Him as Jehovah Shalom (God of peace) if you've never had chaos and confusion in your life? How would you ever know his unspeakable joy if you've never suffered sorrow? How would you know Him as Jehovah Rapha (God who

Heals) if you've never experienced sickness and pain? Last but certainly not least, how would you know Him as ABBA (Daddy, Father) if you've never been fatherless or felt like you were because you were rejected and ignored by your earthly Father? So in closing, if you learn to see yourself the way God sees you, you can learn to love the reflection staring back at you in the mirror. Why? Because you will see that you are fearfully and wonderfully created, a divine craftsmanship (Psalm 139:14) of the Most High God; flaws and all. So let's do some work.

I want you to look in the mirror and stare at yourself for the next five days. This will be extremely hard for some of you, but I promise it will get easier the more you do it. Turn your head from side to side, up and down. Just check yourself out. I know some of you will feel the pressure to look away; fight it! Even if you give in to the pressure, look again! You will feel the urge to skip this part, but this is one of the most important parts. Now, as you stare at yourself, I want you to say out loud what GOD says about you.

Say, God says I'm fearfully and wonderfully created (Psalm 139:14). He loves me with an everlasting love (Jer. 31:3). He declares that the plans that He has for me are to prosper me and not harm me; he will give me a future filled with hope and who can change or frustrate His plans (Jer. 29:11, Isa. 14:27 NASB)? He said I should never be afraid because He will always be with me and never will leave or abandon me (Deut. 31:6), and if God is with and for me, who can be against me (Rom. 8:31)? Because greater is He that's in me than He that is in this world (1 John 4:4)! You can also look up more of what God says about you on your own. You can only fight the enemy with God's Word. Now go in peace, knowing that you are always covered! Remember, do this once a day or more for five days. Don't just wait till you feel bad or things aren't going right.

"You shall have no other gods before me."
Exodus 20:3

Day 13

Today, I Surrender Being "In" Love With Giving

Did you know that anything you give more time, energy, attention, or show favor towards more than your Father in heaven, you have made that thing/person your God? You have literally stepped into idolatry. If we're not careful, we can slip into idolatry and never even know it. Did you know it's possible to make the very thing that God placed and created in you an idol?

Well, here's my story. I've always been a giver. That's how I was created, but what about when you've fallen in love with giving more than the giver (God)? What's even more interesting is when you had no idea how you got there. I knew I had God's heart when it came to giving. I didn't realize that there's a "limit" to what, who, and the amount we should do for and give to others. My idea of having God's heart of giving was to give all I had to anyone that was in need and let God provide my personal needs. Man was I wrong! My discernment was way off. As a matter of fact,

I didn't do much discerning when it came to giving at all back then. One day I was sitting in a friend's car and the Holy Spirit arrested me. He said, "You have the right motives, but you're going about it the wrong way." I said, "God, you made me this way. So how am I doing it wrong?" His response changed the course of my giving and my life from that day forward. He said, "Your money isn't yours; it's mine! You're supposed to ask me who to give to and how much and be ok even if/when I tell you not to help or give at all." I was floored! All this time, I thought I was pleasing God. All I was doing was positioning myself to be used, taken advantage of, and leaving God out of the decision-making process concerning what was rightfully His decision to make.

    I had more questions. I had to know what I needed to do to get in "proper position" to be able to give His way. I kept listening, and He kept talking. "It is out of order, as my child, for you to help prosper everyone else's life, and they see you, in the same situation with no change." I broke down. I couldn't believe all those ignorant prayers I had been praying were insulting to God. "God, whatever you give me, I'll give it all away. "God just bless me enough for me to be comfortable. I don't need to be rich." Just pure unadulterated ignorance! I didn't know any better, and when you don't know, you just don't know. Oh, but God wasn't done with me. He knew with my misguided desire to "give it all away," He needed to drive His point deeper. He said, "When you give away all I give to you, there's no evidence left of me in your life and guess what they're going to say? Look what "Tawanda" has done for us. Not look what I, God, has done." I was so taken back all I could do was say, "I get it, God. I don't want your glory. I'm so sorry! I'm so very sorry. Father, I repent."

    I thought my prayers were pleasing to Him all that time. Unfortunately, they were actually very offensive, not to mention I had inadvertently made myself a glory stealer and an idol worshiper. James 1:17a says, "Every good and perfect gift comes from God." That means

God is the source! He is to us as electricity is to a plug. If you put a plug in a wall outlet, and there's no electricity, there's no power. That's how God is to us. So when we lean on our own understanding and leave Him out of our decisions and plans, we disconnect from the power source.

The gift to give comes from God, not us. So if you're a giver and you've been doing it without God's input, STOP! Ask God who He wants you to give to help, spend time with, or do a favor for? When you let Him in every area of your life, oftentimes, He'll give you discernment about that person and reveal the truth concerning the situation they're presenting to you, sometimes right away and sometimes even before they come to you. Please don't do what I did. There were times even when I knew I heard God say no, and I still did it. I've had to face some harsh consequences because of that, and it is definitely a lesson learned! Don't let your gift of giving make you an idolator and lead you to desire to please people more than God! Ask for wisdom in your giving, wait for an answer, and you can never go wrong.

Are you more in love with the gift than with the giver? Did you know that you have made the gift an idol? I had no idea I was doing any of this, but I thank God for showing me the truth! I've learned my lesson. Will you? If you're ready to do better,

Repeat after me...

Father, your Word says that every good and perfect gift comes from you (James 1:17). Help me always remember that you and you alone are the source of the gift and the talent I possess. Increase my discernment of who to and who not to give my time, energy, resources, and money. Make me sensitive to the guidance of your Holy Spirit so that I won't put myself in situations that will make me an easy target to be used and taken advantage of and increase my desire to please YOU above ALL! In Jesus' name, I pray, Amen.

For God has not given us a spirit of fear and timidity, but of power,
love, and self-discipline.
2 Tim. 1:7 NLT

Day 14

Today, I Surrender Fear

I was always a strong person, but I never liked conflict. If you messed with anyone I loved, you had a serious problem on your hands, especially when it came to my family. But for myself, I wanted to avoid all drama. Why was that? To be honest I really don't know when it started. I don't even know or remember when fear came in and immobilized me so severely that I was able to cheerlead, motivate, encourage, and instruct everyone else on the path to their success but not my own! How did I get here? I asked myself that for years. Was it because I felt unworthy? Was it that I felt like everyone else deserved what God had for them more than I did? Did it come from when I was rejected and mistreated by those closest to me from a very early age? Did it come from the betrayal of those who were supposed to have my back? Or maybe it stemmed from me being so hard on myself, which of course is rooted in rejection. It may have even come from me praying for God to only make me comfortable when it came to financial prosperity. Now you may be asking how does fear have anything to do with that, right? The Bible says in Ecc. 10:19, "...Money answers all things." So if it answers all things in life, good, bad, ugly, and indifferent, then asking for a limited amount means you're fearful of the heights your life can go to if you had an abundance of it because, as the saying goes, "more money, more problems." Some of us don't want to go through anything! We're so comfortable with the small issues of life but don't want to deal with the "oil building" and "faith yielding" issues that it takes to walk in your purpose and calling. We don't realize the stagnation that we created in our own lives. We're so used to first, blaming the devil, settling for what's beneath our purposed destiny, being content with having little, and believing the naysayers when they tell us what we can't do, be, have or accomplish til we place ourselves in the same box we put God in. Let me assure you that God is not like us in His ways or thoughts (Isa. 55:8-9). Some of us are so comfortable in habits and familiarity that we let fear, block, stop, and hinder us from doing God's will, even in the most minor assignments.

The moment God starts speaking to us about how He wants to use us, we're already saying, nope! I can't do that! I'm not qualified to do that. I don't want to move from this place. I don't want to go to another job. I don't want to do anything differently; I'm comfortable right where I am. Or we may say, God, not right now, I have time! You fail to realize that you don't have as much time as you think! God is the author and finisher of our faith, life, and time. He's not in time with us. He's in eternity, not restricted or limited by it like we are. 2 Pet. 3:8 says, "To the Lord, a day is like a thousand years, and a thousand years are like a day." Then who is time really for? If you said us, then you would be correct. God created time for you and I! That's how longsuffering (patient) He is with us.

On top of that, He created us to be incorruptible (in our spirit) just like Him! So, who are we to tell God what we can't do? I heard a pastor on social media say, "Anytime God says something, we want to engage him in a dialogue about our incapabilities! When you only stop to hear part of what God is saying, you will have fear at the introduction without giving God a chance to tell you how the journey will end!" Isn't that good? It's amazing when God reveals the truth about something, and you realize just how jacked up your mindset really was and, for some, still is! It's then that you realize just how much you allowed fear to damage and control so much of your life, which makes you a contributor to helping Satan keep you bound from moving forward or hearing from God. Sometimes and way too often, we question if what we are hearing or seeing is God, to begin with. When you hear something, you blow it off because you don't know, think, or believe it was God's voice you heard. You think it was either you or the devil. I know what I'm talking about because that used to be me! I used to blow stuff off all the time simply because I just didn't know who I was or how God spoke through me.

One day a few years ago, I remember the enemy clearly saying, "You can't hear God." At first, I got angry and then sad, but then a light bulb came on. I thought to myself, wait a minute. Satan is a liar, so if he's speaking, he's lying. Which means he wouldn't have wasted his demonic breath trying to convince me that I couldn't hear from God UNLESS I could. If what he said was true, then wouldn't he want me to stay in the dark about it? He could've just left me thinking what I was already thinking, but instead his lie left room for God to expose and reveal the TRUTH! So I took what he said and SWITCHED it! In other words, what he said I couldn't do was actually highlighting what I could do! Sometimes you have to switch it around on that devil. He can't tell the truth, but because he's a liar, when he says what we can't do, be, and have, it means that you CAN! Now let's deal with the thing that hinders you from being able to switch it up on the enemy, like being "comfortable." I know you feel like the state of being comfortable is safe, but it isn't.

The one thing you don't want to ever do is make God force you out of your comfort zones. I have two words for you IT'S PAINFUL! Trust me on this. Being or wanting to stay comfortable is a dangerous mindset and position. Sometimes we're so stuck in it that any kind of change scares the HELL out of us. One morning, while at work, I said to God that it seems no matter what, there's always going to be either a test from you or temptation from Hell. So if I'm going to go through something anyway, I will no longer allow fear to stop me from being about my Father's business. Right after that, God led me to a Periscope, and on this particular scope, they were quoting 2 Kings 7:4, "If we tell ourselves, 'Let's remain in the city,' we'll die there since there's famine in the city. But if we sit here, we'll still die. So let's go over to the Arameans! If they spare our lives, we'll live, and if they kill us…we're dead anyway!" This gave me so much confirmation, strength, encouragement, and motivation to move forward and never look back.

I felt like God had stood up and yelled, "YES, MY BABY FINALLY GOT IT!" I felt like the lepers in the story; Since I'm going to go through something anyway, in that case, I may as well do it trying to live, be successful, fulfill my obligation of the great commission, get my family delivered and set free, and live out the predestined life that God had already planned for me! From that point on, I felt empowered. Fear had lost its grip, and my faith leveled up. Do not fear; only believe (Mark 5:36)! Now, let's do some work.

What area have you allowed fear to stop you from moving forward? God is saying, "DO IT ANYWAY"! A lot of people don't know that fear is normal! How you ask? Because God made us emotional beings. Fear is an emotion and it is also a spirit. Where we mess up is letting our emotions control us instead of us controlling it, and guess what? We're in great company because Jesus Himself also dealt with fear. Matt. 26:36-46 says that the time had come for Jesus to be crucified. He was so overwhelmed with fear that He went off to pray to the Father three times to ask Him to "take this cup of suffering from me." The cup He was referring to is the pain of being temporarily separated from the Father because he was about to take on the sins of the world. I believe He could handle the physical pain, but being separated from His Father brought him more anguish than anything else He had to face. But thanks be unto God that He finished that verse and completed His assignment even while He was scared! He said, "…Yet not my will, but your will be done." That is how you beat the devil and break fear off your life! The more you put the Father's will before yours, the weaker fear becomes. Is it sinking in? Are you ready to do what Jesus did to prevent fear from stopping you any longer? If you are, then let's pray.

    Father, I now realize that I have let fear stop me from moving in obedience to your will and hold me hostage from walking in my purpose. That stops today! I surrender to you fear, anxiety, worry, stress, and anything else connected to it right now, in Jesus' name. I repent for letting it hinder me in my life. I repent for allowing it to block me from doing, being, and going wherever you were trying to lead me, but more importantly, I repent for allowing it to build a wall in my relationship with you. I declare from here on out that I will move, be, and do whatever it is, even if I'm afraid! Help me to keep my word to you. Your power is made perfect in my weakness (2 Cor. 12:9). Help me to let patience have it's perfect work in me (James 1:4) as I surrender my weakness for your power and my fears and failures for your victories. In Jesus' name, I pray. Amen

14 For if you forgive others when they sin against you, your heavenly Father will also forgive you, 15 but if you do not forgive others their trespasses, neither will your Father forgive your trespasses.
Matt. 6:14-15

Day 15

Today, I Surrender Unforgiveness and the Residue

"Holding a grudge is like drinking poison and waiting for the other person to die." Nelson Mandela

Have you ever heard this quote before? Well, I have. In fact, I lived it! I was a grudge holder for most of my younger life and years into my 20's, and I felt like I had a right to be because of all that I sacrificed, gave, helped, encouraged, and comforted others. HA! What was I thinking? Who did I think I was? I didn't even realize what I was setting myself up for. I was a grudge holder of the worst kind. I didn't just hold grudges against those who hurt me; I also held them against anyone who hurt the people I loved. The offender couldn't come to me at any time afterwards and speak to me because seeing or hearing them took me right back to the original offense, and my response would be, "You know we don't talk!" Well, that was before I knew about the importance of forgiveness. Before

I realized the physical harm, I was doing to myself and the damage I was creating spiritually in my relationship with my heavenly Father. Matt. 6:14-15 simply says that if you don't forgive others for their wrongs towards you, God won't forgive you for your wrongs towards others. This is called supply and demand. In business, supply refers to the amount of available goods. Demand refers to how many people want those goods. As much supply of forgiveness that God has given you, the spiritual definition is that there is a demand in heaven that you also measure out the same to others. I now know that I was operating in the spirit of unforgiveness and experiencing unexplainable pain because of it. The unnecessary stuff I was holding on to created physical illnesses in my body. People who hold on to grudges are more than likely to experience severe depression, post-traumatic stress disorder, and other serious health conditions.

Unforgiveness was killing me slowly but definitely not softly! God created us in His own image, which means if He forgives us and throws it into the sea of forgetfulness, then there's no way we should be holding on to grudges, bitterness, maliciousness, plots of revenge, or anything of the sort (Eph. 4:31-32). When we do, we pay a very high price, not only in our physical health but also our spiritual health as well. Unforgiveness costs us (Matt. 18:21-35) just like forgiveness cost God (John 3:16, Eph. 1:7, Isa.53:5). When I gave my life back to God, that was one of the first things I asked Him to take away from me, and He did just that!

God's deliverance is sometimes so fast and smooth that it takes someone to point out that there's a difference, or God will reveal it so that you can be aware of the change. For example, almost two years after I gave my life back to God, my best friend and I were having a phone conversation. We hadn't talked in all that time, so she didn't know I had gotten saved. We were catching up on everything that happened in our absence, good and bad, and her husband walked in while we talked. He was shocked to learn she was talking to me because it had been so long.

THE TURNAROUND

Before he could say anything, I told her to tell him I said hello! She paused and then told him what I said. He then paused and spoke back. When he walked away, she said, "You have changed!" I said why do you say that? She said, "Because I just told you some really hurtful stuff that he put me through. The "old" Tawanda would've never spoken to him." I told her that Tawanda was dead and that she could expect to see many more changes; it felt good to say that to her. Whom the Son sets free is free indeed (John 8:36)! Are you ready to be free? Can I help set you free today? Let go, let God and let's do some work!

Who in your life are you bitter and anger with? Who do you have negative feelings towards? Name them below. When we surrender people/things to God, naming them out loud is our outward truthful confession not only to God, as well as the enemy. It lets him know that we are serious in our decision to be free and also that we will not stay silent and live in the boundaries of his lies anymore. So name as many as you need to. Then we will pray and be prepared for the Holy Spirit to reveal that you are the real problem in some of these relationships. Remember, the truth sets you free!

1 _____
2 _____
3 _____
4 _____
5 _____
6 _____
7 _____
8 _____
9 _____
10 _____

Father, I forgive (say every name out loud). I surrender to you every negative thought, pain, and issue that I have or ever had with them. I give you permission to come into my heart and mind and snatch out everything that's not like you. Holy Spirit, I ask that you even show me where I'm the problem amongst some of the names and help me humble myself to accept it and allow you to give me wisdom and strategy on how to rectify the issues I have created. I know that I have made the devil mad by boldly making this move, so when he tries to come in and flood me with painful memories, I ask that you come in and raise the standard against him. I continue to confess my forgiveness of them and myself and surrender us to you as many times as I need until there is no more sting. I ask you to move by your spirit in my life and the lives of all that I've named. In Jesus' name. Amen

> But you, O Lord, are a God merciful and gracious, slow to anger and abounding in steadfast love and faithfulness.
> Psalm 86:15 ESV

Day 16

Today, I Surrender The Way I Love

What is your definition of love? Who comes to mind when you think about what love is or an example of what love looks like? Selah

Love is a verb, which means that it is an action word! According to 1 John 3:18 ISV, "We must stop expressing love merely by our words and manner of speech; we must love also in action and in truth." So love isn't silent; love is lived out loud! It isn't inward emotions outwardly expressed through words only; it has to be followed up with an act or deed. Love that does nothing, gives nothing, shows nothing, helps no one, takes no one in, doesn't comfort, doesn't trust, heal, uplift, take care of, encourage, submit to, and yes, even obey isn't love at all! John 14:15 says, "If you love me, you will keep my commandments." So what are God's commandments? In the condensed version, Matt. 22:37-40 says, "Jesus replied, You must love the Lord your God with all your heart, soul, and mind. This is the first and greatest commandment. The second is equally important: Love your neighbor as yourself. On these two commandments depend the whole law and the prophets." So basically, what He's saying is, if you don't love God first and then your neighbor (your friend, your family, loved ones, strangers alike) as you love yourself, then there is an entirely different word for what you're doing because it isn't love.

A lot of times we think we're loving people the right way but we really aren't. It feels right because we love them from the capacity of our own experience of what love is, based on what we were taught and shown. So what if what we were shown is completely opposite of what real love is? God says Love is patient, kind, it doesn't envy, it doesn't boast, it's not proud. It does not dishonor others, it's not self-seeking, it's not easily angered, it keeps no record of wrongs. It doesn't delight in evil but rejoices with the truth. It always protects, always trusts, always hopes, and always perseveres. Love never fails (1 Cor. 13:4-8). Does the way you are showing love look like or sound like that? Also, to shed more light for some of you, love isn't revealed in those ways in the "absence" of conflict but because of it! So, you may be wondering how I know so much about love. According to the revelation that was given to me, my life is a living testimony of Matt. 25:35-40.

Jesus thanked the people for feeding Him when He was hungry, giving Him something to drink when He was thirsty, and inviting Him into their homes. At the same time, while He was yet a stranger, clothed Him when he needed clothes, and visiting and taking care of Him when He was in prison and sick. The people were confused because they didn't remember doing any of that, so they asked, "When did we do all that for you? He replied, "If you did it for the "least of these" my brothers and sisters, you did it for me!" So who are the least that Jesus was referring to? I'm glad you asked; it's the lonely, widowed, orphan, afflicted, abandoned, rejected, hated, falsely accused, brokenhearted and broken-spirited.

So again, how do I know so much about love? Because God took a little girl who was rejected, fatherless, broken, emotionally beaten, who felt worthless, didn't love herself, feared conflict, and thought of herself as lower than others and gave her His heart for His people. I know about love because I live it, and so can you! When I was in my early to mid 20's, I had a long-time boyfriend who did everything for me physically, and I mean in every way you can think of he took care of me. You may be saying, Why is he your "ex"? Because emotionally, he did absolutely nothing for me but wound me. After we broke up, I couldn't understand how he took care of me so well in one way, but hurt me so deeply in another.

God revealed to me that that is what he learned in his family dynamic. They would wound each other with their words. Instead of having a conversation about it, genuinely apologizing, and, most importantly, doing what it takes to not do that again, they would just do something physically for each other like buying a gift, giving a massage, bringing them food, etc. Anything physical but no attempt to heal the emotional wound that was created. God said, "He couldn't give you what he didn't have, so he gave you what he did." So often, we expect others to love us in the same capacity that we love them, but truth be told, some people don't have the ability or capability to do that. Remember, love is an action word (1 John 3:18), but it's also learned and can be taught!

So, who have you deemed unlovable - a family member, friend, or even yourself? I want you to write on one side of a piece of paper all the things you can think of that are good about them or you. It can be a mountain of simple things or one big thing. On the other side, write the bad things.

Repeat after me...

Father, I thank you for loving me even when it was hard for me to love myself and others, let alone you. I thank you that even though

_____ hurt me, you love them just as you love me. Help me to forgive them for real. Reveal more good things about them so I can see that it outweighs the bad. Reveal the good in the things that I think are bad and help me move out of the way so that you can love them through me. In Jesus' name. Amen.

Now, wait in silence for 10 minutes to see if you hear anything. You may hear something right way, or you might hear something along the way, but don't stop listening and asking until you get a response. Most importantly, don't limit God or put him in a box. He reveals answers through anything and anyone! So don't just listen or look for the obvious! God is not predictable.

Then he walked another whole day into the desert. Finally, he came to a large tree and sat down in it's shade. He begged the Lord, "I've had enough! Just let me die!
1 Kings 19:4 CEV

Day 17

Today, I Surrender The Hard Place

Have you ever been in a hard place before? Have you ever felt like Elijah and said, "I've had enough"? Have you ever experienced circumstances that made you want to throw in the towel and let the chips fall where they may? Yeah, I've been there too. It is the loneliest, most vulnerable, fearful, and anxiety ridden place I've ever been in. Hard places of deep despair that leave us dazed, confused, and feeling abandoned and unprotected turns our world inside out. It creates irrational thoughts like God has forgotten about you and doesn't care what happens to you.

Here's my story. There was a period when I was going through so much that I literally should have died! We owned our building in the mid-'90s to early 2000's, and my apartment was completely taken over by mold by the end of our living there. I had fought this battle for years doing everything I could to get rid of it. I tried all sorts of products, natural remedies, having the building worked on inside and out, and getting grants and loans to remedy the issue, but nothing worked. They all were just temporary reliefs. I was sick all the time. I had throat, sinus, ear, and viral infections. Before we moved there, I didn't even so much as snore, let alone get sick. The majority of the time my family didn't even know I was sick because I was such a homebody. I loved being in my place by myself. But this place that I had called home for eighteen years had slowly become a death chamber. I was sick and tired of being sick! I begged God to help me. I had done all that was in my power to do, and I was completely depleted; at one point, I gave up. No one on the outside knew it but my house showed it. I literally felt like I was the walking dead as my health slowly deteriorated. I had started living like a vagrant in my own home. I stopped cleaning up, I stopped trying to get rid of the mold, and anyone that knows me knows that I love a clean house. I was tired, sick and I felt like God had abandoned me.

It was enough to make you take yourself out, and nobody knew what was going on because I wouldn't let anyone in my house. So, after I did all I could and resolved within myself that God had forgotten about me, I gave up and waited to die. God finally got me out of that situation. We eventually moved out but I still to this day am dealing with a few of the health issues as a result of living in that building. When I look back on all that I had gone through, I'm left with only one thought; But by the grace of God, I am still here! Obviously, God had a purpose for me. I should have died. Anyone that knows about mold knows that it kills. I should not have lived eighteen long years like that and lived to tell it. When I think about all the hell my body endured, yet still in good working order, I can't help but give God praise. What would have taken anyone else out; I survived. Thank you, Jesus! In our humanity, we search for any reason why this and that happened. We look for anyone other than ourselves to point the finger at. In our lack of understanding, we often make God the main and sometimes the only target of our blame.

Has it ever dawned on you that God had nothing to do with some of the things that you're accusing him of? Have you ever considered that you are the reason you're in that position, and God never intended any of that for you? Yes, He knew it would happen, but do you know there's a silver lining for every storm? For every test, there's a strategy, and for every trial, there's a testimony! Has it ever come to mind that God is just as hurt as you are, watching you go through so much? You don't even realize how much God loves you, do you? Maybe it's time that you found out just like I had to. In 1 Kings 19:7-8, God loved Elijah so much that when he was depleted and pleaded with him to just let him die, he sent an angel to feed him, give him a drink and strengthen him to keep going. What God allows or sends is not to harm you but to bring you to your already planned, ordered, and expected end (Jer. 29:11). Your pain, loss, and sacrifice are purposed. Your suffering wasn't and isn't in vain. So, you can't give up now. You've come too far to turn around at this stage. So, stay the course and watch God move.

What is or was your hard place? Do you know why you had to go through that? Did you ask God? If so, did he give you an answer? Are you struggling with why you had to go through so much? Why did it have to hurt so bad? Why did it have to be that person? Trust me when I say God hears your silent and outward questions. He knows your heart and thoughts before they enter your mind (Psalm 139:1-2). Nothing can be hidden from him (Heb. 4:13). So, if you haven't already done so, you may as well let Him in. He knows all about it anyway. Are you ready to surrender your hard places to God and trust Him with your deepest pain and darkest secrets? It's not a secret to Him, but He wants you to permit him to help you! Sometimes our situations and circumstances leave us so guarded that we don't trust anyone, not even God, our creator. Beloved, it's time to heal, let go, face your fears, forgive, and receive/accept forgiveness. In other words, it is time to grow up, level up, and give the enemy the boot! It's time. God is waiting on you. I want you to stand up, reach out your hand as though you're reaching for God's hand, and start walking. Walk around your house as you read this prayer.

Father, I surrender my hard place to you. I surrender the situations and the people attached to them and every trouble and pain connected to them. Help me to let go? Help me to forgive them and myself? Help me to lay down what's left of me and my life at this point and reach up and grab the life that you have had waiting for me all along. Please help me to know and see that the pain was purposed and that it was/is preparation for what you have in store for me. Father, save me from my enemies, even if the enemy you save me from is me! I give you permission to come in and have your way as I accept your help of letting you into every area of my life.

Remove the guards, break down the walls and help me to see myself as you see me as I follow your lead into my new life and next level. Satan you have no more authority or power over me, my house, or my life. I command you to cease and desist right now! GET OUT IN JESUS NAME! You are no longer welcome here! God and I got this from here on out (now go to the door, open it, and keep praying). I hereby cancel every subscription and agreement I've ever made with Hell. It's time for you to go and never return, in Jesus' name.

Now slam that door, and welcome to FREEDOM!

25 "Therefore I tell you, do not worry about your life, what you will eat or drink; or about your body, what you will wear. Is not life more than food, and the body more than clothes? 26 Look at the birds. They don't plant or harvest or store food in barns, for your heavenly Father feeds them. And aren't you far more valuable to him than they are? 27 Can all your worries add a single moment to your life?....
30 Why do you have such little faith?"
Matt. 6:25-27, 30 NIV, NLT

Day 18

Today, I Surrender Worrying

"Worrying is like a rocking chair, it gives you something to do, but it gets you nowhere." Glenn Turner

Sometimes the most common sense quotes are the most life changing. That's what this quote did for me when I first read it years ago because I used to be a worrier which was one of those nasty little generational curses I inherited from my mom. If it was small, I made it huge, and if it was huge, I made it gigantic! Did you know that worrying is a sin? It warps your thinking and taints your trust in God. It creates doubt about everything and anybody and you become a complete basket case, living in a constant state of fear. How do I know? Because I lived it, and on top of everything, I was making myself sick because "stress kills!"

I'm living proof that that's not just a popular quote used to get people to take high priced meds to pad the pharmaceutical company's pockets.

After having so much unexplainable pain in my body, I finally went to the doctor. After a few x-rays, tests, and follow-up appointments, the doctor asked me, "Why are you carrying so much at such a young age?" I responded, "What did you see that made you ask me that?" He told me that stress was eating away at my insides, which was creating all my pain. Now, I still don't know how he could see that. Technology back then wasn't as advanced as today, so how could he know? I thought that maybe he had many of these same cases, and it was easily recognizable. I honestly don't know, but I do know that he was spot on in what he saw and said. Worrying is a dream stealer and faith killer! Because it robs you of so much precious time, thus hindering you from living life!

So many of us deal with worry and anxiety, which is usually rooted in fear (Matt. 6:34)! God is the author and finisher of our faith (Heb. 12:2). So why do we worry about the future? Simply put, It's a trick of the enemy to get you to doubt God. If he can create doubt in you about what God says in His Word, then he can control how you view and think about it! So maybe all of your worry is because you're looking at your future through a distorted lens. Heb. 11:1 says, "Faith is the substance of things hoped for, and the evidence of things not seen." 2 Cor. 5:7 says, "We walk by faith, not by sight." To sum the two up together, what God is saying is, Faith takes what you hope for, which is invisible, and makes it visible and tangible so that you can touch it; if you walk out your life based on what you believe, according to my word, not what you can see. Did that help make it clear for you? So if Satan can distort what you believe about what God's Word says, that makes it easier for you to believe his lies. It's the same thing he did to Eve in the garden (Gen. 1:6).

He convinced her that eating from the tree that Adam was given clear instructions not to eat from, the tree of the knowledge of good and evil, wasn't going to really kill them like God said it would (Gen. 2:16-17). God didn't tell Adam not to eat from it because He was mean and stingy; he created everything he would ever need to live before He created Adam. He didn't want them to eat from that particular tree because he loved them so much that he never wanted them to know evil. He never wanted us to know lack, know what it feels like to be broke, busted, and disgusted. He never wanted us to know sadness or pain of any kind, and guess what else? He never even created us to die! I believe he was teaching Adam obedience. Sure, he could have made it impossible for them to even get to the tree, but he gave Adam the "freedom of choice."

God doesn't want a bunch of mindless puppets. He wanted them to choose to be obedient to Him. It's the same for us today. He still gives us free will because He wants us to choose Him! He wants us to obey Him out of love because we would feel like prisoners without a choice, and our obedience would be obligational and forced. God wants us, just like He did with Adam and Eve, to choose to obey Him and reap the benefits He's waiting to bless us with (James 1:12). Guess what? Your worrying is blocking God from blessing you. If we would only gather enough faith the size of a tiny mustard seed (Luke 17:6), He would bless us! So, are you ready to stop worrying and put your trust in God? Are you prepared to surrender to Him by casting all your worries, doubts, and cares on Him so that He can show you how much He cares for you (1 Pet. 5:7)? Matt. 11:28 says, "Come to me, all of you who are weary and carry heavy burdens, and I will give you rest." Aren't you tired of carrying your burdens? Do you want God's rest? If you are ready, then

Repeat after me…

Father, I have given up too much of my time and life worrying about things I cannot control. I have put my trust in things and people that mean me no good. I know now that all I had to do was trust you to fight my battles. The enemy may have won the battle far too long, but I surrender the victory of the war to you. I surrender my mind, actions, fear, second-guessing, indecisiveness, and anything else connected and associated with worry. I repent for not trusting you from the beginning and doubting what your Word says. I hereby declare that I'm using my weapon, which is your Word, when I'm tempted to worry! It is written that eyes have not seen, ears have not heard, nor has it entered our minds what you have in store for those that love you, and if I'm going to continue worrying, I may never see any of this! I trade anxiety for your peace, I trade doubt for your faith, and I trade my time for your time. Move by your Spirit to get me in line with heaven. In Jesus' name. Amen

I can do all things through CHRIST who strengthens me.
Phil. 4:13

Day 19

Today, I Surrender To Letting God Be God - Part 1

"I'm Only Doing What You Ask Me To Do." God

    This is what God said to me one day when I questioned Him about what I thought was a very unfair move at my job. So often, we pray to God for things and have our own expectations of how we think He's going to answer. In my 48 years of living, I can say that God has never answered my prayers the way I thought He would. I've learned that there's absolutely nothing predictable about God. There are countless mysteries about Him, and I've experienced only a few of them. I'm sure you have too whether you know it or not.

    Here's my story. There are actually two parts to this story; this is the first part. At the time, I had been at my job for almost 26 years, and 15 of those years were spent in one building. I loved everything about that building. The structure of it, the people, and especially the students, but by the end of 2016 into 2017 there were so many things going on around me that it made it impossible to focus on any one thing. It also made my personal time that I usually spend with God impossible because other things and people were taking up that time, and I felt like my relationship with Him was suffering. It had gotten so bad that I cried out to God and simply said, "Father, remove all of the distractions!" My supervisor came to me a few months later and said they were transferring me effective immediately. I had the most seniority in the building and almost on the entire East Campus for my department, yet I was the one chosen to be moved. I didn't even ask why because I didn't believe that they would be honest with me. I was so hurt and angry that I didn't even want to talk to anyone in the new building. When I took my first break, I went somewhere private, and I broke down. I asked God, "Why did you let them move me? There are so many other people they could've moved! Why would you let them do that to me?" Confused and angry at my job and partially at God, I felt completely thrown away.

While I was crying uncontrollably, I heard clearly, "I'm only doing what you asked me to do!" Now, even more confused, I said, "What did I say that would make you allow them to do this to me?" He then reminded me about my prayer to remove the distractions. I was floored and completely embarrassed. I repented profusely as I felt like the biggest fool. I could've asked Him why I was the one that was moved and not the distraction, but what difference would it have made at that point? Obviously, He had His reasons for moving me, and because I know Him, this had to be for my good, right?

Well, it didn't feel like it at the time, but after I calmed down and allowed myself to lean on His peace, I started thinking they couldn't be honest with me because it was God who moved them to do what they did. They didn't even know what was happening. Sometimes, His answer to our prayers looks and feels like He's completely against us. It feels like you are being punished for something you did, and you have no idea what it is that you did. Let me assure you that nothing God does is to harm you (Jer. 29:11). We don't always understand His ways, but I've learned that we're not supposed to; we're just supposed to trust Him no matter what. Who would want to serve a God that you can figure out? Who would serve a God whose every move can be predicted? I can truly say that although it hurt, moving me was the best move to make. I have more than enough uninterrupted time with God now, and that is what I prayed for, not to mention that so many other things are beneficial for me where I am now.

What if God put me here to help someone else? What if what He put in me was needed by someone in the new building? How do I know that this move wasn't already part of His plan? What if He was using the distractions to make me so uncomfortable that it led me to pray the prayer that ultimately led me to unknowingly pray for His will to be done? What if, just what if I had gotten too comfortable where I was? God will do whatever He needs to do to ensure that we go from being comfortable to usable! He knows that comfortability creates a dangerous level of laziness, thus making it impossible for us to move to the level of obedience that He needs from us. He only did what I asked Him to do. Wow! Has God ever said that to you? Has He ever answered your prayer in a completely unpredictable way, and it made you feel like He was against you? Did it make you feel like He cared about everyone else but you? Do you now realize that it was the best move to make, and in that, He showed you just how much He loves you and that He cares about what you care about down to the smallest details (Psalm 37:23)? Did you repent for doubting Him? I did, and if you haven't already, then it's time.

Repeat after me...

God, there were so many times when I thought you were against me. I now realize that it was me that was wrong. Wrong for putting limitations on you. Wrong for putting you in a box and wrong for treating you like you were on the same level as me. I'm so sorry for ever doubting you. When I don't understand your ways, help me move from flesh to faith, help me to not lean on my feeble-minded understanding, and let you direct my path (Prov. 3:5-6). Help me to let you be true, and every man/woman be a liar (Rom. 3:4), including myself, so that my trust in you guides me into all truth (John 16:13). Set me free with the reality of who you are, making me who I am. Move in my life not by your power, or might but by your spirit (Zech 4:1) so that my trust is without borders (Psalm 107:28-30). I repent. I'm so sorry. I surrender to your way, your Word, and your will. In Jesus' name. Amen.

The steps of a good man are ordered by the Lord: and he delights in his ways.
Psalm 37:23 KJV

Day 20

Today, I Surrender To Letting God Be GOD - Part 2

"I'm Only Doing What You Ask Me To Do." God

So, by this time, I've been in the new building for a few months, and I'm adjusting to my new assignment and co-workers. Still, as you remember, my first day was emotionally stressful because I didn't want to talk to or be around anyone. It was easy for me to get away for some uninterrupted alone time with God. That should have been my first indication that this was a "God" move since that had become the issue in the other building, but I digress. I was being so standoffish towards the guy training me that he speedily walked me through my new assignment. He didn't turn on any lights because he was used to only relying on the light from the exit signs and the street lights coming through the windows. The next day it was my turn to do it on my own and even though I had a few stumbles, I did a pretty good job based on what I remembered. Eventually, my eyes adjusted to the glimmer of light that led my path in and out of each area til I would only turn on the lights when it was time to do detailed work. One day, as I was entering a particular area (on a side that I usually didn't come in on because it is usually dark), it was lit up, and the side that's usually lit up was dark. I stopped dead in my tracks, looked around for a few minutes, and said, "God, why is it bright on this side of the room, darker on the other side, and why is this sticking out to me?" I stood there for a few minutes to listen, then returned to my work. Suddenly, I heard, "You've gotten used to walking in the dark." Wait! What does that have to do with the new lighting arrangement? Is what I asked out loud as I chuckled. I was reminded of how I had to be trained to adjust to the dark because I didn't know where the light switches were initially. So I used that same path that I had been taught to walk in until it became familiar.

    I'd gotten so comfortable in familiarity that He had to redirect my steps. He told me, "I have to redirect your steps by making the path you were used to going in darker so that you couldn't find it anymore, and I highlighted the path that I wanted you to walk in, to keep you, not just on track, but on the right track." That is how much God loves us, and that's also the danger of becoming comfortable in dysfunction, pain, suffering, generational curses, in darkness, etc. We learn to adapt to whatever situation and circumstance we're in until something comes in and creates an atmosphere so extremely uncomfortable, making it impossible to stay there any longer. It makes the place that we created a comfortable spot no longer bearable. I was completely outdone. It takes moments like that to make you realize just how much God loves you and just how much you're on His mind. How encouraging, I thought to myself. God cares enough about me to ensure I'm always in His will. Have you ever had one of those moments that God just came right in and flipped your life upside down so that you could learn to walk and live right side up? I repented for not turning to Him in times of trouble and for letting myself be overcome by what was going on around me. God speaks in so many different ways. Don't put Him in a box. Have you recognized anything different sticking out in your normal routine? Watch, listen, expect the unexpected and

Repeat after me…

Father, today I surrender to walk in the path of the "predestined" steps that you have laid out for me according to Psalm 37:23 and as I surrender to your will and way for my life, help me to stay on track even and especially when all hell is breaking loose around me. Your Word says that you are a very present help in trouble (Psalm 46:1), so in those times, help me lean on you and not unto my understanding (Prov. 3:5-6). Help me not follow in the footsteps of the generations before me but pick up my cross and follow your Son daily (Luke 9:23). Remove the scales off of my eyes so that I may be able to see your truth amid the darkness that I have become accustomed to. I come out of agreement with the curses on my bloodline and into agreement with the blood of Jesus that was shed for the forgiveness of my sins (Matt. 26:28). I dedicate or rededicate my life back to you to have full control coupled with my full cooperation. It is in your Son's mighty and matchless name, I pray. Amen

3 For what if some did not believe? shall their unbelief make the faith of God without effect? 4 Not at all! Let God be true, and every human being a liar. As it is written: "So that you may be proved right when you speak and prevail when you are judged."
Rom. 3:3-4

Day 21

Today, I Surrender Being Right

Have you ever been in a position wherein you thought you were completely right about something and when you found out that you were wrong, your desire to stay right was so deep that you fought against the truth no matter the cost? Are you one of those people that just absolutely hates being wrong? It's so bad that you are willing to hide and cover up the truth so that it never gets revealed. Well, if this is you let me say this, you are treading on dangerously thin ice. God's Word says, "You shall know the truth and the truth will set you free." (John 8:32). If you desire to be right in the eyes of people even and especially over the freedom that comes from God's truth, then you are operating in a hazardous level of pride. If you continue in that mindset, you are setting yourself up for destruction and a fall (Prov. 16:18).

Pride is dangerous not only because God Himself hates it (Prov. 8:13), but also because it distorts the view of ourselves by painting our personal sin as a beautiful portrait of innocence in the sight of God and everyone else's as filthy and unforgivable.

Some of us despise being wrong and cannot deal with it, mainly because we're so accustomed to being right a lot of the time. But when your love for God and His ways are stronger than the false reputation that you create in the eyes of men, you will realize that being wrong is a humbling experience, and if you're willing, your confession of the truth brings breakthrough to someone else.

Here's a perfect example. There's a pastor I met on social media; at that time, I had been following him for almost a year. God gave him a word one day, and he hopped online to share it with us. In the short version, he said, "I heard the Lord say that He's giving His people double grace. Then he reminded me that today is May 5th, 5 - 5. Five is the number of Grace. God wants to give you double for every area of your life (mentally, emotionally, physically, financially, and spiritually). Make sure you get a $55 seed in the ground today!" He came on again later to further declare double grace to God's people, and he said," If you don't have it today, then tomorrow will be too late." Now because I've gotten in trouble with God about my giving in the past, I asked Him, am I one of the ones that should sow? I felt I received confirmation in my spirit to do it, but I didn't move right away because I wanted to make sure it was God speaking and not me being high in my emotions because of the powerful word. The way that God usually speaks to me is through repetition. So finally, after a few confirmations, I made up my mind to do it. Still, I didn't do it right away because I got distracted, and before I knew it, I fell asleep. After a few hours, I jumped up out of my sleep in a panic and said, "Oh my God, I didn't sow my seed!!!" Still half asleep, I was trying to focus on the time, but it was blurry. I thought I saw 11:16 pm, which meant that it was before midnight and I would still be on time to sow before the day ended, and I prayed, "Father, please let that say 11:16 pm and not 1:16 am!" My focus finally became clear, and the clock did in fact, say 1:16 am. I was heartbroken. I was so distraught that it took me over an hour and a half to go back to sleep. When I finally fell asleep, God spoke to me in a dream and said, "Sow your seed." I said, "But God, so and so said if we didn't do it yesterday, it'll be too late." What He said next will stick with me for the rest of my life. In His effort to ensure that I received His confirmation over anyone else's, He said in the firmest yet gentlest voice, "I'm God!" I jumped out of my dream, sowed my seed, and the note I attached to it was, "My seed for double grace. He said it's not too late."

When the Man of God came back on social media that day, I asked him did he receive my seed and my note? His initial response was, yes, but what he said next is one of the reasons why I believe, as a leader, he is so greatly respected. He said, "Tawanda, I read what you said, and I took it to God!" (selah). He said, "God, you said yesterday was 5 – 5, today is 5 – 6, and God said to me I told you it started yesterday, I didn't say it stopped yesterday!" This statement blew my mind because I hesitated to send the note with my seed. I didn't hesitate to write what it was for, but I almost didn't write that God said it's not too late, and because I did, that made him go back and seek Him for clarity. Did you catch that? Some people may have taken him, saying that after today, it's too late, as him being manipulative because there are many who do that. But because God had revealed His heart to me not just for him but also towards His people, I simply looked at it for what it was, human error. What I've learned in this whole Christian journey is, we need to stop telling God what people said and start telling people what God said! He could have not gone back to God and just left it as is, but because he humbled himself and cared more about the truth than being right in his initial statement, I believe he created a space for breakthrough for his followers and viewers that day. It also left room for others to sow, now that they knew it wasn't too late, so they too may be the recipients of the double grace blessing. He cared more about the people getting what God had for them above anything else even more than being right. That is how you determine the quantity and quality of God in people. Would you have come back and did that? Would you have been willing to come back just as publicly as you did initially and say, "Hold on guys, God corrected me, and here's what he said?" If you wouldn't have, then you need to repent and surrender every morsel of that pride to God.

There are so many lessons and revelations to receive when He shows us what area we were wrong in, and it builds up not only a good reputation and respect from others when you admit it, but it also pleases God and counts you as being trustworthy. Not only that, but it also opens the door to God's favor in your life! One of the most rewarding statements to ever hear in your life is that God trusts you! I don't know about you, but it's being trusted by God for me ALL DAY, EVERY DAY! No other opinion matters when you have God's stamp of approval. Do you desire God's approval over anyone else's? If it didn't matter to you before, but after reading this, you have a change of heart, then

Repeat after me...

Father, I confess today that I have valued man's opinion and approval of me more than yours. I repent for caring more about being wrong in their eyes than I did about being right and pleasing in yours! I realize now that I have been operating from the spirit of pride, and I surrender it, and everything connected to it to you on today. Help me to see myself the way you see me. Not the way my family, friends, strangers and enemies alike, but the way you, being my creator and my Father, sees me. Help me to know the truth, accept the freedom that comes with it and walk in it boldly. I surrender the parts of me that I don't want people to know and see to you so that when I must expose them, I will do it without fear. Fear of rejection, condemnation, and without fear of their faces (Jer. 1:8). In Jesus' merciful, patient, and understanding name, I pray. Amen

THE TURNAROUND

QUESTIONS and ANSWERS

I know for some of you, that was a lot, but guess what? You made it! Give a loud hand clap to congratulate yourself. Go ahead and do it until you get tired. Sometimes we don't give ourselves enough credit. It's ok to give yourself a pat on the back and say good job, and I'm proud of you. We've been taught to put ourselves down for so long that even when we do something that should be commended, we minimize it by saying all that we should have done differently! Stop that and clap for yourself! You deserve it! Now, this is where you get to see how far you have come in these 21 days. Let's journey back for a minute. Are you ready? Let's go!

1. What story or stories helped you the most and why?

_____
_____
_____
_____
_____
_____
_____
_____
_____
_____

2. What story helped you gain a greater understanding and revelation about yourself? Why you act the way that you act and why you are the way that you are.

3. What story helped you, if you are already a believer, realize that you desire and need a more personal and intimate relationship with God?

4. If you're not a believer, which story made you want to be and moved you to give your life to God and why?

5. What story made you realize that you've been doing and handling so many things, people and life in general the wrong way but now you want to learn how to do it God's way?

6.   What story made you want to let go of bitterness and anger and accept forgiveness and forgive? It not only taught you the importance of forgiving others but also forgive yourself.

_____
_____
_____
_____
_____
_____
_____
_____
_____
_____
_____
_____
_____
_____
_____
_____
_____

7.   What story impacted you so much so that you will never forget it and you will share it so that it can help others as well?

_____
_____

8. What story gave you the greatest revelation that God is real and that He loves you and wants you to receive nothing less than His best?

www.ingramcontent.com/pod-product-compliance
Lightning Source LLC
Chambersburg PA
CBHW080446110426
42743CB00016B/3297